D0225799

# TELEVISION COVERAGE
# OF THE MIDDLE EAST

# COMMUNICATION AND INFORMATION SCIENCE

A series of monographs, treatises, and texts

Edited by
**MELVIN J. VOIGT**
*University of California, San Diego*

Hewitt D. Crane • The New Social Marketplace: Notes on Effecting Social Change in America's Third Century

Rhonda J. Crane • The Politics of International Standards: France and the Color TV War

Herbert S. Dordick, Helen G. Bradley, and Burt Nanus • The Emerging Network Marketplace

Glen Fisher • American Communication in a Global Society

Bradley S. Greenberg • Life on Television: Content Analyses of US TV Drama

John S. Lawrence and Bernard M. Timberg • Fair Use and Free Inquiry: Copyright Law and the New Media

Robert G. Meadow • Politics as Communication

William H. Melody, Liora R. Salter, and Paul Heyer • Culture, Communication, and Dependency: The Tradition of H.A. Innis

Vincent Mosco • Broadcasting in the United States: Innovative Challenge and Organizational Control

Kaarle Nordenstreng and Herbert I. Schiller • National Sovereignty and International Communication: A Reader

*Forthcoming titles by William C. Adams include:*

*Television Coverage of International Affairs*
*Television Coverage of the 1980 Campaign*

In Preparation:

Ithiel de Sola Pool • Retrospective Technology Assessment of the Telephone
Robert M. Landau • Emerging Office Systems
Kaarle Nordenstreng • The Mass Media Declaration of UNESCO
Herbert I. Schiller • Who Knows: Information in the Age of the Fortune 500
Claire K. Schultz • Computer History and Information Access
Osmo Wiio • Information and Communication Systems

# TELEVISION COVERAGE
# OF THE MIDDLE EAST

**William C. Adams**
*George Washington University*

ABLEX Publishing Corporation
Norwood, New Jersey 07648

**Library of Congress Cataloging in Publication Data**
Main entry under title:

Television Coverage of the Middle East.

   (Communication and information science)
   Includes indexes.
   1. Near East—Politics and government—1945-
2. Television broadcasting of news—United States.
I. Adams, William C.   II. Series.
DS63.1.T44      956'.04     81-15049
ISBN 0-89391-083-X      AACR2

ABLEX Publishing Corporation
355 Chestnut Street
Norwood, New Jersey 07648

# CONTENTS

# PREFACE

During the 1970s, the Middle East became the dominant focus of international news coverage on US television. Although Americans have come to rely heavily on the networks for foreign news, little systematic research has been published on coverage of the Middle East. In the past, the topic of reporting on this volatile region has been subjected to polemics more than to scholarly analysis. To address the latter, this volume brings together eight previously unpublished studies of television's treatment of the Middle East and examines a wide range of issues and events.

In the first chapter, William Adams and Phillip Heyl analyze patterns in covering individual countries in the region from 1972 through 1980, and summarize the content findings of later chapters and show correlations with public opinion; Adams and Heyl also discuss in detail the particular patterns of coverage of Afghanistan and Iran.

The five chapters that follow are about various aspects of coverage of Israel and Arab nations. Robert Lichter reports on the attitudes of elite broadcast and print journalists toward the US commitment to Israel. Magda Bagnied and Steven Schneider have assessed the coverage of Sadat's trip to Jerusalem. Morad Asi summarizes the findings of a major time-series content analysis of Middle Eastern news. Itzhak Roeh reviews the structure of stories about Israeli activity in southern Lebanon. And, Jack Shaheen considers the portrayal of Saudis and Palestinians in several important network documentaries.

The final two chapters concern the epic news stories of late 1979 and 1980—the Soviet occupation of Afghanistan and the American hostages in

Tehran. Montague Kern has investigated the use of domestic and foreign sources in reporting Afghanistan. David Altheide has explored the viewpoints and omissions in TV news accounts of the hostage crisis.

The contributors to this volume have brought a broad range of experience, perspectives, and methods to the study of television news reporting of the Middle East. Their chapters represent the culmination of many hours of careful content analysis and study. Their enthusiasm for this book and their cooperation in its assembly are deeply appreciated.

A number of colleagues at George Washington University have also been very supportive of this effort. Dean Burton Sapin of the School of Public and International Affairs, David Pollock of the Political Science Department, and David Brown, Michael Harmon, and Charles Washington of the Public Administration Department have provided encouragement and advice. Other George Washington friends and associates who helped in a variety of ways include Karen Bland, Phil Heyl, Bellen Joyner, Vanessa Barnes, Karen Arrington, Margaret Sheehan, Fay Schreibman, Jim Steadman, Linda Trageser, and perhaps Michael Robinson. Brad Bryen and Martin Kirkwood were excellent research assistants. It was a pleasure to work with Lucia Read, Barbara Bernstein, and Karen Siletti at Ablex. Thanks also go to Martha Glass, Kathy Reed, Charles Reed, Wilma Adams, and Robert Darcy. The volume is dedicated to Prof. Lyle C. Brown of Baylor University, an extraordinary scholar and teacher.

William Adams
July 1, 1981

# CONTRIBUTORS

**WILLIAM ADAMS** is associate professor of public administration at George Washington University, co-editor of *Television Network News: Issues in Content Research*, and editor of *Television Coverage of International Affairs* and *Television Coverage of the 1980 Campaign.*

**DAVID ALTHEIDE** is associate professor of sociology at Arizona State University. His books on the media include *Creating Reality: How TV News Distorts Events, Bureaucratic Politics,* and *Media Logic,* and he has authored numerous essays for scholarly journals.

**MORAD ASI** directs the journalism program at Al-Najah National University in Nablus on the West Bank. He served in the U.S. Army as a reporter-photographer for American military publications in Europe, was awarded a foreign correspondent internship with the Associated Press in Cyprus in 1979, and earned his Ph.D. in mass communication from Ohio University in 1981.

**MAGDA BAGNIED** analyzed U.S. television coverage of Sadat's trip to Jerusalem for her Ph.D. dissertation at Cairo University. She also has a M.A. in mass communication from the American University in Cairo; from 1976–78, she worked as a researcher for the ABC news bureau in Cairo and was later employed as a production assistant with the NBC news bureau in Cairo.

**PHILLIP HEYL** teaches political science at the Coast Guard Academy in New London, Conn., and earned his Master of Public Administration degree from George Washington University.

**MONTAGUE KERN** recently completed her Ph.D. at the Johns Hopkins School of Advanced International Studies. She is co-author of a forthcoming volume, *The Press, the Presidency and Foreign Policy: The Kennedy Years.*

**S. ROBERT LICHTER** is assistant professor of political science at George Washington University and Senior Fellow at the Research Institute on International Change at Columbia University. He is co-author of *Radical Christians, Radical Jews,* numerous articles on political activism, and a forthcoming volume on elite journalists.

**ITZHAK ROEH,** a senior news editor and anchorman for Israeli television, is also on the faculty of the Communications Institute of the Hebrew University of Jerusalem. Dr. Roeh earned his Ph.D. in communication from Columbia University and is co-author of *Almost Midnight: Reforming the Late Night News.*

**STEVEN SCHNEIDER** is a graduate student at the Annenberg School of Communication, University of Pennsylvania, and holds a B.A. in political communication from George Washington University. His earlier study of coverage of Sadat's trip to Jerusalem was published in Richard Cole's *Introduction to Political Inquiry.*

**JACK SHAHEEN** is professor of mass communication at Southern Illinois University, Edwardsville. Dr. Shaheen has been a Fulbright Scholar at American University, Beirut, and the University of Jordan, Amman. He edited *Nuclear War Films* and is author of a forthcoming book tentatively titled *Arabia on Television.*

# TELEVISION COVERAGE
# OF THE MIDDLE EAST

# 1

## FROM CAIRO TO KABUL
## WITH THE NETWORKS, 1972–1980

### WILLIAM ADAMS
### PHILLIP HEYL

On the outskirts of Dayton, Ohio, lives a forty-seven-year-old housewife whose husband is a machinist. She has a high school education, a part-time job, two children, and attends a Protestant church. Her neighbors are not aware that she was actually invented by two political analysts (Scammon & Wattenberg, 1970) as the prototypical American "Middle Voter."

Her swings in voting—from Johnson to Nixon to Carter to Reagan— have been thoroughly chronicled, along with her opinions on a wide range of subjects. Much less is known about how she forms her impressions of the changing world scene.

At least three nights a week she sits with her husband to watch local and national television news. They go to a couple of movies each year, and last year she found time to read a paperback book recommended by a friend. They subscribe to a Dayton newspaper, which—amid household chores, job, kids, cooking, and church—she tries to look at each day. The paper is small enough that she can usually manage to glance through it almost every day, although Landers gets more attention than Kraft, Will, and Reston.

A year or so earlier, when a Roper pollster had asked for her main source of "news about what's going on in the world today," she had replied "television," as had about two-thirds of those surveyed.[1] In particular, she said she relied on TV for international news.

---

[1] Some of the statistically "typical" characteristics added to Scammon and Wattenberg's hypothetical Dayton woman are drawn from Sterling and Haight (1978).

Her answer was not too surprising. The local papers devoted little space to international news, except during crises, and she found television's stories more vivid and usually fairly easy to follow. It seemed to her as if most of what she tried to recall about foreign affairs was associated with pictures she has seen on television.

As she watched television during the 1970s, she had seen its international focus replace one corner of Asia—the Southeast—with another corner of Asia—the Middle East. It became the new Vietnam, the new setting which seemed to be the crucible of the US foreign concerns.

She watched a parade of invasions, wars, religious turmoil, terrorism, economic crises, revolutions, summits, and periodically renewed hopes for peace. Broadcast news bore a certain resemblance to a print account of the same region which she read at her church—the Old Testament. Whatever the gulf that separated Cronkite's reports from those of Moses, she would not have thought Cronkite's accounts of the region were any less accurate.

What did the woman in Dayton and her counterparts across the country watch and learn about the Middle East on television news—and why should we care? The reasons for being interested in the content of Middle East news are many. Extensive coverage may elevate a Middle East issue to a high spot in the national consciousness and to a high priority on the national policy agenda (e.g., hostages in Iran, Soviet occupation of Afghanistan). Ignoring certain Middle East stories may leave intact whatever policy inertia was already in place (e.g., Iran and Afghanistan in mid-1979).

Coverage may also lift selected leaders and countries—and their perspectives—to greater prominence, and the character of that coverage may make them more or less sympathetic (cf., Sadat and Egypt; Begin and Israel; Arafat and the PLO). News of the Middle East may influence attitudes toward US foreign policy in general as well as views toward the world as a "dangerous place" requiring armed might rather than conciliation. However, even if the Dayton housewife should have opinions on the Middle East that are not at all influenced by her reliance on TV news, political leaders in Washington, Cairo, Tel-Aviv, and Tehran believe that television does influence her, and they package their activities accordingly.

There are other reasons to be concerned about television's treatment of the Middle East besides its potential impact on public opinion and on political elites. The reigning US "news culture" dictates that news ought to be as accurate, as fair, and as thorough as possible. Evaluating news coverage on such criteria can be an end in itself, quite apart from its degree of influence.

Some analysts attempt to determine how particular organizational, technological, legal, and commercial factors act to shape the content of news. To assess the role of such factors, more information is needed about patterns in actual news content.

Very little systematic research has been published on media coverage of the Middle East. A few studies have been conducted about newspaper and magazine coverage (Belkaoui, 1978; Suleiman, 1965, 1970; Terry, 1971, 1974; Wagner, 1973; Padelford, 1979; see also Hadar, 1980; Feith, 1980), and even less has been published involving content analysis of television coverage of the Middle East (Gordon, 1975; Mishra, 1979). (On international news coverage generally see Adams, 1981; Gerbner & Marvanyi, 1977; Larson, 1979; Lent, 1977; Rubin, 1977; Batscha, 1975.)

What were viewers in Dayton and elsewhere being shown about news from Cairo to Kabul? With the goal of better understanding television's pictures of the Middle East, this volume brings together a wide range of original research by scholars who have various perspectives and methodologies. This chapter is intended to provide an overview of network coverage of the entire region from 1972 through 1980, with special attention to the unusual coverage of Iran in 1979–80. After describing the methodology, we present a summary of the Middle East on the TV news agenda from 1972 through 1980, discuss parallel trends in US public opinion, review the treatment of Afghanistan, and conclude with an examination of coverage of the hostages in Tehran, its volume, impetus, and repercussions.


## METHODOLOGY

We did not use a sample. We reviewed the agenda of every weekday broadcast from January 1972 through December 1980 of the ABC, CBS, and NBC networks' early evening, flagship news programs. Working at George Washington University's Gelman Library, we used Vanderbilt's *Television News Index and Abstracts* to identify all of the stories related to the Middle East.

The purposes of the exercise were to measure the emphasis given all Middle East news across this nine-year period and to measure the patterns in coverage of countries in the region. The total time for each story was partitioned among the key countries in the story. For example, stories about the Camp David Summit were allocated one-third each to the United States, Israel, and Egypt; a story about the Iraq-Iran war would be coded with one-half of the seconds to Iran and one-half to Iraq.

The United States, the Soviet Union, and other countries were also coded when they appeared in stories about the Middle East. The region was extended to include Afghanistan which, as will be explained later, the networks treated as part of the Middle East. In addition to distributing news time among countries, there were also categories for the United Nations, for OPEC and the "Arab world," and for Palestinians and the PLO.

Some additional coding conventions should be noted: Stories about individuals were allotted to their home country, so Begin, for example, was always coded as "Israel" and the Shah was still coded as "Iran" after he left the country. Entirely peripheral references were not coded; a story about the Ayatollah Khomeini in exile was coded as "Iran" if his presence in France was not integral to the story. Multinational corporations were coded according to the country of their headquarters.

A story about "Palestinian forces in Lebanon raided by Israeli commandos" would be coded to give one-third of the time to the Palestinians, one-third to Lebanon, and one-third to Israel. Obviously, this is arbitrary in the sense that the proportions are imprecise. We found this approach to be useful, however, for several reasons. First, it provides a cumulative measure. Time given all countries and groups can be added to equal "total Middle East news time." Second, at least some of that imprecision, though not all, is likely to even out over time; that is, some stories about Lebanon and Syria may stress Syria, while others may emphasize Lebanon. Third, the time for a story entirely about one nation is allocated to that nation totally, while time for a story about a number of countries is divided among those countries. Thus, the measure offers a good indication of the relative amount of coverage nations and others received on the network news from 1972 through 1980.

## THE REGION AND THE NETWORKS, 1972–1980

The networks paid relatively little attention to events in the Middle East in 1972. Although tensions were high, the Middle East was a much lower priority than Vietnam, China, and the Soviet Union. On an average weeknight in 1972, CBS gave Middle East news only thirty seconds of air time. The most dominant theme was that of terrorism and sporadic violence —plane hijackings, the murder of Israeli athletes at the Munich Olympics (Leebron, 1978), terrorism at Tel-Aviv's airport, Israeli offensives in southern Lebanon and Syria, and miscellaneous other stories. However, 1972 was the last year the Middle East had low visibility on network news. The following year, the Middle East began to compete with Vietnam as the most prominent international area.

In 1973, Middle East coverage tripled over that in 1972. On an average weeknight in 1973, CBS gave the region nearly 1 minute 40 seconds of news time. Coverage of raids and terrorism continued, but the news explosion came with the October 1973 war. The war's aftermath, the Geneva Peace Conference, OPEC and the Arab oil embargo, disengagement activities and disputes (along with continued raids, Maalot, and terrorism) sustained the fairly high level of attention into 1974. CBS gave the Middle East an average of nearly 2 minutes of news time each weeknight in 1974.

Coverage decreased slightly in 1975 and 1976, while stories centered on a wide range of developments, including Kissinger's shuttle diplomacy, continued border fighting, Entebbe, hijackings, and other topics. The civil war in Lebanon dominated 1976 coverage. CBS had an average of just over 1½ minutes of Middle East coverage each weeknight in 1975, and nearly 1¾ minutes per weeknight newscast in 1976.

By television standards, the Middle East had attained a high degree of attention. Each newscast usually has fewer than twenty-three minutes of actual news time, so during the 1973–76 period between 7 and 9 percent of total news time was devoted to coverage of the Middle East. It was during this period that the Middle East supplanted southeast Asia as the center of foreign news coverage, the networks expanded their Middle Eastern bureaus, and Arab leaders began to accommodate Western media (Mosettig & Griggs, 1980).

The view became widespread that the 1973 war and oil embargo had been the turning point for a reorientation of Western media toward greater concern with the region, for increased interest in Arab news and opinions, and for a growing awareness of the situation of the Palestinians (Sreebny, 1979; "Interviews," 1976). Our data do confirm that the October 1973 war marked the beginning of heightened coverage of the Middle East, although there is little evidence, either in our study or in others in this volume, that 1973 marked a shift toward more "pro-Arab" coverage, a subject to which we will return.

The greater change in the volume of coverage came in 1977, and from 1977 through the end of 1980 the Middle East thoroughly consumed most of television's coverage of international affairs. In 1977, TV news gave increased priority to such stories as the US president's meetings with Middle East chiefs of state, Cyrus Vance's travels in the region, elections in Israel and Begin's victory, OPEC oil price increases, fighting in Lebanon, and US policy toward the PLO. The biggest story that year was Anwar Sadat's trip to Jerusalem and its reverberations. The trip was given saturation coverage for several weeks and quickly made Sadat a well-known and popular figure. In 1977, CBS averaged over 2 minutes 10 seconds of Middle East news each weeknight—almost 10 percent of the nightly newscast, a figure that continued to increase in the following years.

TV news in 1978 followed-up on the "peace initiative" story with news of negotiations and the US role, amid reports of fighting in Lebanon, bombings, and terrorism. In early autumn, television had its third blockbuster event—the Camp David Summit of Carter, Begin, and Sadat. Middle East news in 1978 increased to an average of 3 minutes 8 seconds each weeknight on CBS.

Coverage escalated still further in 1979. The overthrow of the Shah of Iran early in the year, Egyptian-Israeli negotiations and treaty, Begin's visit to Egypt, Andrew Young's meeting with the PLO, oil price increases, and many other stories had already made 1979 another year of extensive Middle

East coverage, when, on November fourth, the US Embassy in Tehran was seized. Over the entire year, CBS had an average of 4 minutes 33 seconds each weeknight about the Middle East—roughly 20 percent of all newstime.

That the Middle East received one-fifth of all the nightly news on CBS —slightly more on ABC, slightly less on NBC—was extraordinary. By way of comparison, it is more coverage than the Vietnam War and negotiations received in 1972 or that Watergate received in 1973 (Lefever, 1974). Certainly no other area of international affairs seriously rivaled the Middle East for TV news attention in the late 1970s.

Middle East coverage increased once more in 1980. CBS had an average of 5 minutes 10 seconds of stories about the region on the weeknight newscasts—about 23 percent of all newstime. The bulk of the coverage was about the American hostages in Tehran and about the Soviet occupation of Afghanistan, and to a lesser extent about the Iran-Iraq war.

So extensive was Iranian and Afghan news that, coupled with the presidental campaign, and events in Poland, Italy, Miami, Oregon, and the Florida Keys, news from the rest of the Middle East was displaced. Despite important developments in the Arab-Israeli relations, relatively little time was devoted to the subject compared to the "new" Middle East stories. Continued disagreements between Egypt and Israel, strained American-Israeli relations, bombings and other problems on the West Bank, and a variety of other significant stories competed with an already overcrowded list of Middle East stories. So, paradoxically, the year of the most Middle East news, 1980, was so overwhelmed by news from Iran and Afghanistan that the usual focus on the Arab-Israeli conflict was lost.

These general patterns from 1972 through 1980 were evidenced on all three networks. Table 1.1 shows the totals of Middle East coverage for each of the networks over the nine years. As studies almost always find, the networks maintained a persistent uniformity in their agendas. With the sole exception of NBC's decline in the total time given Middle East news be-

**Table 1.1**
**Minutes of Middle East Coverage**
**on Weeknight Network News, 1972–1980**

|      | ABC | CBS | NBC |
|------|-----|-----|-----|
| 1972 | 177.5 | 131.7 | 177.2 |
| 1973 | 484.9 | 427.9 | 438.8 |
| 1974 | 567.4 | 502.4 | 526.8 |
| 1975 | 370.8 | 401.5 | 407.4 |
| 1976 | 383.4 | 448.3 | 313.5 |
| 1977 | 509.7 | 571.0 | 419.8 |
| 1978 | 792.9 | 816.0 | 691.7 |
| 1979 | 1,209.2 | 1,182.3 | 1,051.6 |
| 1980 | 1,432.7 | 1,341.2 | 1,116.7 |

tween 1975 and 1976, when ABC and CBS increased coverage, the networks covaried from year to year.

In the early period from 1972 through 1974, ABC offered the most Middle East news; in 1975, NBC held a brief lead. From 1976 through 1978, CBS was out front, with ABC providing the most coverage in 1979 and 1980. Since 1976, NBC has had the least Middle East coverage of the networks, a finding that may be attributed to the network's general tendency to focus more on domestic news and to its "Special Segment" features which are usually on domestic stories. *ABC's World News Tonight* has become especially likely to emphasize international stories. Nonetheless, the key finding is in the network similarities rather than the small differences.

The basic patterns were repeated on all three networks. Having previously been relegated to infrequent coverage, the Middle East surfaced as a high priority news arena after the 1973 war. Sustaining attention to the Middle East during the middle 1970s, the networks devoted nearly 10 percent of their newscasts to the region. Then came a succession of epic events—Sadat's trip to Jerusalem in 1977, the Camp David Summit in 1978, the downfall of the Shah of Iran in 1979, and the hostage crisis and occupation of Afghanistan in 1979–80. For several years, almost one-fifth and sometimes over one-fith of the nightly newscasts directly concerned the Middle East—quite a record for a medium that is accused of downplaying foreign news (Gans, 1980) and of focusing on routine news (Epstein, 1973).

As television paid increasing attention to all Middle East news, it bore in on a few selected events and gave them saturation coverage. To appreciate the approach of TV news to these events, it is first necessary to consider its approach to big stories generally.

Television news is not so much an "electronic front page" (as is often claimed) as it is an electronic caricature of newspapers. A big story may consume the totality of a nightly newscast, out of proportion to the "front page" analogy. During the height of a crisis, newspaper front pages are still likely to have proportionately more non-crisis news than TV news. News on television is relatively more engulfed by the crisis story. If the entire public affairs section of the newspaper is considered, the newspaper would have far more non-crisis news than television.

The networks tend to pick up a key story and follow it as a continuing saga. With an episode such as the hostages in Tehran, this translates into sustained, saturation coverage night after night—sometimes without regard for the presence of tangible developments.

Six stories stand out in TV news coverage as having received intense coverage for an extended period of time. No other events rivaled these six stories:

1. the October 1973 Arab-Israeli war and oil embargo
2. Anwar Sadat's trip to Jerusalem in November 1977

3. the Camp David Summit with Carter, Begin, and Sadat in September 1978
4. the fall of the Shah and Iranian Revolution in early 1979
5. the American hostages in Iran, November 1979–January 1981
6. the Soviet occupation of Afghanistan in the winter of 1980

All six stories were rather startling and publicly unanticipated developments. Wars, civil wars, and invasions appear to be the strongest candidates for massive coverage. The 1973 war, the Iranian Revolution, and the Soviets in Afghanistan all made the list of top stories, and the hostage seizure could well be called "warlike." (Similarly, the two stories which ranked seventh and eighth during this period were the Lebanese civil war in 1976 and the Iran-Iraq war in 1980.) Two unusually peaceful events were also given saturation coverage—Sadat's Jerusalem visit and the Camp David Summit.

All six of these stories received large amounts of television coverage, although coverage of the hostage story dwarfed all others. Later in this chapter, we will further consider the volume of coverage given the Iranian crisis. Other contributors to this volume analyze three of these major stories: Magda Bagnied and Steven Schneider on Sadat's trip (Chapter 3), Montague Kern on Afghanistan (Chapter 7), and David Altheide on Iran (Chapter 8). Elsewhere Gordon (1975) examined coverage of the 1973 war, and William Spragens has conducted research on coverage of Camp David.

Such stories are of special interest to political communication scholars because they seem more likely to be interpreted and repeatedly emphasized as pivotal events by subsequent media and political analyses, seem more likely to be capable of altering existing perceptions and more likely to be embedded in the audience's memory, and perhaps to be more likely to influence the course of events through immediate feedback (see Oberdorfer, 1979; Kraus *et al.*, 1975; Graber, 1980, pp. 225–269).

These saturation stories substantially reorient news shows by reducing the already small number of different news items aired to only a handful of quick headlines, while the lead and most of the program consists of news about the "epic" event. Bagnied and Schneider show, for example, what coverage of this magnitude meant for Sadat's trip to Jerusalem: continuous extensive play as the lead story for many days prior to the visit; saturation coverage, displacing almost all other news, during the actual visit; and long follow-up stories for many days after the visit; along with news specials and live coverage. The perceived importance bestowed by such coverage clearly elevates the "news value" of later, derivative stories. Coverage of Sadat's Jerusalem visit epitomized what had been happening in a less dramatic fashion to general coverage of Middle East news in the 1970s on all three networks: The region was receiving more attention than ever before and, as will be explained in the section that follows, that attention focused on the Arab-Israeli conflict.

## NATIONS ON TV NEWS, 1972–1980

The methodology described earlier is especially suited for a nation by nation comparison of amounts of Middle East news time. What parts of the region were given extensive coverage? What countries were overlooked?

Table 1.2 presents the allocation of minutes of news time over the 1972–1980 period. These total annual times are the averages of ABC, CBS, and NBC, so Table 1.2 shows the number of minutes that the "average network" gave various countries and groups in the Middle East for each of the nine years. (As noted already, network trends were highly correlated.)

Table 1.2
Minutes of Weeknight News Time
on the "Average Network" on all Weeknight Newscasts,
1972–80 (Average of ABC, CBS, and NBC)

|  | 1972 | 1973 | 1974 | 1975 | 1976 | 1977 | 1978 | 1979 | 1980 |
|---|---|---|---|---|---|---|---|---|---|
| Israel | 46.5 | 123.8 | 112.9 | 79.2 | 56.4 | 129.2 | 185.5 | 107.4 | 44.7 |
| Egypt | 10.1 | 61.3 | 36.2 | 57.3 | 14.8 | 69.4 | 142.7 | 72.7 | 27.8 |
| USA | 16.9 | 69.9 | 112.4 | 84.5 | 46.7 | 94.4 | 162.4 | 352.3 | 434.4 |
| PLO | 24.5 | 26.6 | 36.8 | 19.9 | 54.2 | 45.6 | 61.7 | 55.0 | 20.8 |
| Lebanon | 5.5 | 9.2 | 12.6 | 48.5 | 84.8 | 18.3 | 37.8 | 12.6 | 2.4 |
| Syria | 5.1 | 34.3 | 47.9 | 11.4 | 36.9 | 20.3 | 15.4 | 3.5 | 5.2 |
| Jordan | 5.2 | 5.8 | 9.7 | 4.4 | 4.6 | 17.3 | 16.4 | 4.7 | 8.4 |
| S. Arabia | —— | 10.4 | 14.4 | 15.1 | 7.4 | 6.5 | 21.5 | 25.0 | 13.7 |
| Iran | 4.6 | 2.2 | 5.2 | 5.5 | 4.0 | 9.8 | 54.7 | 381.7 | 368.9 |
| Afghanistan | —— | .6 | —— | —— | —— | —— | 1.4 | 10.1 | 65.1 |
| Iraq | 1.1 | 1.6 | 1.3 | .4 | 1.4 | 1.6 | 4.2 | 3.5 | 49.3 |
| Yemen | .7 | —— | .1 | —— | —— | .4 | .7 | 2.1 | 1.0 |
| Kuwait | —— | 4.1 | 2.3 | .6 | .4 | .8 | .1 | 1.3 | .8 |
| Oman | —— | —— | —— | —— | .4 | —— | —— | .3 | 3.1 |
| Emirates | —— | —— | .3 | .1 | .6 | .7 | .6 | .7 | 1.1 |
| Libya | 2.4 | 6.0 | 2.3 | 1.1 | 3.0 | 4.9 | 3.0 | 5.3 | 50.4 |
| Algeria | —— | 1.6 | 1.8 | .5 | .5 | 1.2 | .7 | .7 | 10.6 |
| Tunisia | .1 | .1 | 1.4 | —— | —— | .6 | —— | —— | —— |
| USSR | 8.0 | 22.7 | 12.6 | 7.5 | 5.2 | 12.3 | 11.4 | 20.5 | 74.2 |
| Europe | 14.0 | 19.3 | 14.3 | 7.7 | 9.4 | 8.5 | 9.6 | 9.9 | 24.0 |
| UN | 3.9 | 13.2 | 23.3 | 13.5 | 9.3 | 9.5 | 14.6 | 24.4 | 42.3 |
| OPEC/Arab | 6.3 | 22.4 | 24.7 | 20.5 | 27.5 | 22.7 | 9.7 | 20.7 | 8.3 |
| Middle East | .3 | 4.3 | 10.2 | 12.9 | 5.6 | 5.0 | 3.2 | 2.5 | 3.6 |
| Other | 7.0 | 11.3 | 49.2 | 2.6 | 8.7 | 21.5 | 9.6 | 30.7 | 36.6 |

Several broad patterns in the data in Table 1.2 should be emphasized. US television networks gave:

1. extremely low levels of coverage of small Arabian-peninsula nations
2. very low levels of most Arab states in north Africa
3. very low levels of Iran (prior to 1978) and of Iraq and Afghanistan (prior to 1980)
4. most attention to Israel
5. relatively high levels of coverage of Arab states that border Israel, and of the PLO
6. declining coverage of Israel as a proportion of the coverage given to Egypt and the PLO
7. substantially different coverage in 1980, which can be attributed to coverage of the hostage crisis
8. an emphasis on American relations with the Middle East, with less notice of Soviet, European, or United Nations activities.

### Arabian Peninsula

Around the borders of Saudi Arabia are a number of states that are small in terms of geography and population, but that produce nearly one-tenth of the world's output of oil. Kuwait, Qatar, Bahrein, Oman, the Yemens, and the Emirates did not receive serious attention at any time during the nine-year period. During most years, all of these states together received less than 3 minutes of coverage over twelve month periods. They received the most coverage in 1980—6 minutes in all.

Apparently, when these states act most powerfully in international affairs, they are subsumed into "OPEC"—the Organization of Petroleum Exporting Countries. In news of OPEC, these states are seldom mentioned by name, nor are they mentioned for their role in OPEC, their relations with the United States, or their internal politics.

Saudi Arabia has obtained the most coverage of the states on the Arabian peninsula, with special notice given its role as a "moderate" in OPEC and as a friend of the United States. (Jack Shaheen evaluates network documentaries about the Saudis in Chapter 6). In 1978 and 1979, as the presumably stable regime in Iran began to crumble, the networks began to look a bit closer at the presumably stable regime in Saudi Arabia.

The most surprising finding with regard to coverage of states on the Arabian peninsula is not so much the inattention to the small states on the Gulf or the greater (though still modest) focus on the Saudis, but rather the undiscovered war in Yemen.

During the 1970s small-scale fighting erupted off and on between the Yemen Arab Republic ("North Yemen") and the Yemen People's Democratic Republic ("South Yemen"). President al-Ghashmi of North Yemen was assassinated in July 1978, and the severity of border clashes grew. The fighting escalated to open warfare in February and March 1979. President Carter sent a squadron of F-15 fighters and US warships to the general area, and the Defense Department confirmed that US military personnel were being sent to North Yemen, along with millions of dollars of tanks, artillery, and other weapons.

Despite these developments and the geographically strategic location, the networks gave only minimal coverage. In February, CBS had two very brief weeknight stories on the fighting, NBC had one, and ABC none. In March, each network had 4 or 5 brief stories.

Remarkably enough, both North and South Yemen were getting weapons from the USSR by the end of 1979, although no mention was made of this arms deal by the networks in November or December. Also not mentioned was the success of further Soviet initiatives with South Yemen or the Soviet-Yemen PDR treaty of October 1979.

### North Africa

With the exception of Egypt, the Arab states north of the Sahara got low levels of coverage during the 1970s. Libya, Tunisia, Algeria, and Morocco had only slightly more news time than did the small states of the Arabian peninsula.

Matters changed in 1980 when the president's brother, Billy Carter, became closely linked with the government of Libya. Coverage of Libya became almost ten times what it had been. The scandal with Billy Carter— complete with Congressional hearings, charges of "cover up," repeatedly amended versions of events, and a colorful leading character—was an irresistible television story. Libya was presented, sometimes almost in passing, as a despicable, outlaw country with a key role supporting international terrorism.

Coverage of Billy Carter and Libya in 1980 accentuated the extent to which Libya had usually been disregarded. In the years 1972 through 1979, Libya had typically received only 3½ minutes of coverage over an entire year. During that same period, international terrorism—airplane hijackings, bombings, assassinations, kidnappings—had been given massive coverage on TV news. Nevertheless, the country presented in 1980 as a linchpin for such activities, providing arms, ammunition, training, funds, sanctuary, and often open endorsement of acts of terrorism, had been ignored in all the preceding years. Had Billy Carter's understanding of Libya been based on television news?

### Tigris to Khyber

As with most Arabian peninsula and north African states, Iraq, Iran, and Afghanistan received very low levels of coverage during most of the

1970s. Many years passed with Afghanistan getting no coverage at all. Iraq received very little coverage, usually less than two minutes a year, until the 1980 war with Iran.

The remarkably low level of news time given Iran prior to 1978 is of special interest. Despite the vast scale of US military aid to Iran and the Shah's central role in the US Middle East strategy, Iran received an average of just over 5 minutes a year from 1972 through 1977 on the "average network" weeknight newscasts. During the downfall of the Shah, coverage of Iran burgeoned, and with the taking of American hostages, Iran overshadowed all else in the Middle East for over 14½ months.

Coverage of both Iran and Afghanistan is discussed later in this chapter and in other essays in this book. Iran and Afghanistan are cited here, along with Iraq, to underscore their similarities with most of the small Arabian-peninsula and north African states: In addition to having received relatively low levels of TV news coverage, they do not border Israel.

## Israel

The hub of Middle East coverage has been Israel. News from the region has largely been defined in terms of Israel's perils. Arab states that border Israel have consequently received more attention than the rest of the Arab world. Appreciating the extent to which Middle East news became synonymous with news of the Arab-Israeli conflict helps explain many of the findings from Table 1.2.

Stories that are not directly related to the Arab-Israeli conflict—the Yemenite war, the machinations of Libya's Kaddafi, internal events in Iran, the initial pro-Soviet coup in Afghanistan—appear to be screened out as less newsworthy. Such stories seem to be very minor distractions to the primary story of Israel's survival.

Robert Lichter's study in Chapter 2 shows that leading broadcast and print journalists overwhelmingly support a strong American commitment to the survival of Israel. It is certainly consistent with Lichter's finding that Israel's relations with adjacent states would be given the highest priority in Middle East coverage, sometimes at the expense of other subjects.

Only a few stories broke the Israeli-Arab focus to a significant degree: the Lebanese civil war, the fall of the Shah, the taking of American hostages, and the Soviet occupation of Afghanistan. While these latter three subjects radically revised the regional news priorities in 1979 and 1980, "Israel and neighbors" was the standard fare.[2]

In almost every year, Israel received more coverage than any other Middle Eastern state. International relations stories tended to involve Israel

[2] Adams and Ferber (1977) analyzed *Meet the Press, Face the Nation,* and *Issues and Answers* from 1965 through 1974 and found that Ambassadors and Prime Ministers of Israel were given 38 programs. In contrast, Egyptian representatives participated in only 12 shows; Jordan, 9; Iran, 2; Syria, 1; Saudi Arabia, 1; and the PLO, 1.

and Egypt, Israel and Syria, Israel and Jordan, etc. Coverage of the bordering states usually concerned relations with Israel; early coverage of the Lebanese civil war came closest to being a major exception, although later coverage more explicitly linked Israel to this story too.

At the beginning of the 1970s, the Arab states were ill-prepared to communicate with the networks. The main network bureaus were in Israel. Arab leaders usually refused to allow American television access and made little effort to accommodate Western media, much less to try to effect a positive media image.

Some of the studies in this volume suggest that by the end of the 1970s, television news offered a considerably different approach to Middle East coverage. It was more critical of Israel, and more receptive to Egyptian and even Palestinian viewpoints, although not substantially changed toward the rest of the Arab states. These findings are consistent with our agenda data inasmuch as Israel's news time, as a proportion of the time devoted to Egypt and Palestinians, declined considerably during these years.

All three networks combined gave Egypt only 43 percent as much news time as was given to Israel from 1972 through 1976. From 1977 (the year of Sadat's trip) through 1980, however, the networks gave Egypt 67 percent as much time as Israel. A decline in the relative amount of news time for Israel can also be found if the time alloted news about the PLO is added to that given Egypt. In the 1972–76 period, Palestinian and Egyptian news time was 86 percent that of Israel, while, in the 1977–80 period, it was 107 percent that of Israel. Asi's study in Chapter 4 indicates that not only were Egypt and Palestinians obtaining more coverage relative to that of Israel, but getting more favorable coverage after 1977. Our reading of coverage also suggests that Palestinians were less linked to terrorism in stories during the later period.

Overall, the stress on the Arab-Israeli conflict has skewed Middle East news away from the parts of the region that are not contiguous to Israel. At the same time, emphasis on the US policy and its role has skewed news away from the relations of the rest of the world to the Middle East, especially the Soviets, Europeans, and the United Nations.

## Invisible Soviets, Europeans, and UN

International news anywhere in the world tends to be ethnocentric. Foremost, people are concerned about their own country and its place in the world. In the United States, "international relations" usually means "bilateral relations" between the US and any other country.

Events that link two other countries but do not directly involve the United States seem inherently less newsworthy; war or the imminent threat of war is necessary to secure any large amount of coverage. US-French relations and US-Syrian relations, for example, far outrank French-Syrian relations. Some sort of violence would probably be needed to prompt much news about the interactions of France and Syria—or Iran and Iraq, or Greece and Turkey, or Libya and Chad.

If this supposition holds true in Middle East coverage, the network news departments would typically overlook most stories about the Soviet Union's activities in the region, about European states' policies toward the region, and about United Nations connections with the Middle East. In fact, this was the case. There were only three near exceptions (where coverage exceeded fifteen minutes per network over a combined three-month period): the Soviet Union vis-a-vis the 1973 war, the Soviet occupation of Afghanistan, and the United Nations involvement with the hostage crisis. These episodes still had much American response and involvement and also support the war-and-ethnocentrism interpretation of non-US news. When international relations involve neither a war nor the US State Department, how can it be significant?

What does TV news miss by this particular blindspot? A few examples will illustrate the consequences. Libya's Kaddafi journeyed to Moscow and sharply realigned his nation in May of 1974, a far-reaching move that was surprising in view of Kaddafi's past anti-communism. The networks missed the story altogether.

In the early 1970s, Brezhnev moved further to support elements in the PLO. The PLO formally opened an office in Moscow in August 1974. As Heikal (1978, p. 269) put it: "For the Soviets, the Palestinian movement offered certain very real advantages. It could well turn out to be the time bomb which would upset the prospects of a pax Americana for the area." The early, crucial Soviet attachment to the PLO was little more than alluded to by the networks.

In 1972, despite near total dependence on the Soviets for arms and aid, Anwar Sadat expelled Soviet military advisors from Egypt. In the face of the vast significance this held for a possible radical restructuring of Egyptian policies—and consequently for the entire Middle East—the networks gave the story only passing notice. CBS and ABC spent less than 3 minutes on the subject; NBC gave it 4½ minutes.

Between 1972 and 1976, the Soviet Union delivered over twice as much military aid to selected countries of the Middle East as it gave to all the countries of Africa, Latin America (including Cuba), and South Asia combined—an estimated seven billion dollars in (largely unnewsworthy) weapons.

The networks did report the abrogation of the Soviet-Egyptian Treaty of Friendship in March of 1976, although by this point relations between the two countries had already deteriorated. There was also some attention to the Soviet Union in the early autumn of 1977 at the time of the joint Soviet-American statement calling for a settlement that would insure "the legitimate rights of the Palestinians" and calling for a resumption of the Geneva peace conference. Again, the America connection made the story more newsworthy. This joint action was the last major mention of the Soviet Union and the Middle East until Soviet troops landed in Kabul.

If the United States is not directly involved and the State Department is not issuing a stream of statements, or if war or violence is not yet imminent, relations between the nations of the Middle East and the Soviets, Europeans, and United Nations are given only the briefest mention, if noted at all. Consistent with their coverage of calamitous events, the networks will be sure to cover an Iran-Iraq war or an overt Soviet invasion. More subtle exchanges will rarely get attention, especially if the State Department is silent. The Europeans may provide an occasional Greek chorus in reaction to American initiatives, but their unique relations with the Middle East are not newsworthy. Perhaps the strongest illustration of this practice is to compare the coverage given Afghanistan's "quiet" take-over by a Soviet-backed regime with coverage months later in the introduction of Soviet tanks and soldiers.

Until the events in Afghanistan and Iran in 1979 and 1980, Middle East news was mostly about the Arab-Israeli conflict and the US role in the region. With the patterns of coverage reviewed here, we can turn to trends in public opinion about the Arab-Israeli conflict which may be influenced by this coverage.

## PUBLIC OPINION AND COVERAGE
## OF THE ARAB-ISRAELI CONFLICT

Middle East leaders have come to appreciate the importance of popular attitudes in setting limits on US foreign policy. They are increasingly sensitive to their treatment in US media and clearly want to have a favorable image in the eyes of Americans. Chaim Herzog of Israel said (Benjamin, 1975, p. 52): "The main battlefield now is the theater of opinion in the United States." What has been happening on that battlefield?

Articles in this volume are aimed at analyzing the content of television news coverage of the Middle East. The key findings of these studies would predict some notable changes in public opinion. What was the impact of TV news content on public opinion? Given the conclusions of these studies, what more can be said about popular views on the Arab-Israeli conflict?

The extent to which television news can and does influence public opinion is the subject of continuing scholarly debate (see Comstock et al., 1978; Adams, 1978; Graber, 1980). The old idea that media effects are trivial has been increasingly reexamined and rejected or reformulated. We do not have data available that would allow us a strict measure of how much the content patterns reported in this volume were "assimilated" by the viewing public. We can, however, use some time series data from Gallup polls to determine whether trends in public opinion[3] were consistent with trends in television coverage.

Do opinion trends mirror TV trends? If there is a correlation, it would still not be sufficient proof that television news content "caused" the shifts, but we would have established one of the elements necessary to make such an inference. On the other hand, if TV content does not correlate with public attitudes, it would be possible to reject the idea of a relationship. At least we can see if the proposition can withstand an attempt to falsify it.

Mere correlations between public opinion shifts and television coverage do not permit an examination of the dynamics through which media messages are received and interpreted. Rather, this approach supposes that media messages may be associated with "net" national impacts, whatever the panoply of social contexts and individual uses of the media. It should also be noted that simple correlations cannot distinguish between television and newspaper messages. To the degree their messages are similar, changes in public opinion may be a product of both.

From among the many content findings in this volume, there are five broad conclusions regarding coverage of the Arab-Israeli conflict that can be compared with national responses to Gallup poll questions. If media messages helped mold public opinion, we would expect Americans to have changed in five important respects:

1. more favorable to Egypt
2. more sensitive to differences among Arab nations
3. less favorable to Israel
4. more sympathetic to Palestinians
5. slightly more pro-Arab overall

These are highly charged issues, and are anything but trivial. For each topic, we will first summarize why the data would predict a change in a particular direction, and go on to see if public opinion did coincide with TV news.

### Favorable Images of Egypt

One of the major reversals in the 1970s was the televised image of Egypt. Researchers appear unanimous in the view that Sadat and his nation became the beneficiaries of enormously more favorable coverage.

Some observers argued that Sadat was portrayed as more "moderate" than he deserved (Rubin, 1975; Feith, 1980); others charged that he was covered positively only because he was "overly accommodating" toward Israel. We are not debating whether Sadat and Egypt "deserved" better treatment. The direction of coverage can be analyzed apart from its merits

---

[3] Previous reports on public opinion on the Arab-Israeli conflict include Erskine (1969), Gruen (1975), Lipset and Schneider (1977), Kohut (1978), Raab (1974), and Ibrahim (1974).

and appropriateness, and coverage of Egypt did swing toward a more positive perspective.

Bagnied and Schneider found that Sadat was given intensely favorable treatment during his trip to Jerusalem in 1977. Asi found that Sadat, other Egyptian leaders, and the state of Egypt received overwhelmingly favorable or at least neutral coverage in 1979; prior to Sadat's trip, Egypt's coverage was much more negative. In terms of sheer quantity of coverage, we noted earlier an increase in the amount of attention to Egypt, relative to that given Israel during and after 1977. These findings add up to a straightforward prediction that public opinion since 1976 should have grown more favorable toward Egypt.

Gallup surveys indicate that Americans increasingly liked Egypt. In June 1976, 46 percent were favorable, while 39 percent were unfavorable (and 12 percent had no opinion). In 3½ years, the segment favoring Egypt increased 22 percentage points. By January 1980, fully 71 percent of the Americans surveyed had a positive view of Egypt, while only 23 percent were negative (with 6 percent having no opinion). Thus, by 1980, Egypt's rating had advanced to a ratio of 3:1, pro–con.

The polls also showed a large increase in the proportion of people who are "highly favorable" toward Egypt. The Gallup surveys asked respondents to rate nations on a scale of $+5$ (very favorable) to $-5$ (very unfavorable). In 1976, only 14 percent of the total sample was highly favorable toward Egypt (ratings $+5$, $+4$, $+3$). In 1980, one-third (34 percent) were highly favorable toward Egypt. In this instance, the clear-cut change in the direction and intensity of public opinion paralleled television's picture of Egypt and Sadat.

## Distinctions Among Arab Countries

One finding that emerges repeatedly from the studies in this book is that, during the 1970s, network news came to distinguish among Arab states, and to treat them less as an undifferentiated, unified bloc. The most remarkable case was that of Egypt. Bagnied and Schneider observe that coverage of Sadat's trip to Jerusalem continually stressed Egypt's uniqueness and the hostility of certain other Arab nations. Supporting this point precisely, Asi's time series shows coverage of Egypt changing considerably from that given other key Arab states.

Shaheen reviews network documentaries that address the special cultures and problems of the Saudis and of the Palestinians. While there may be growing emphasis on the distinctiveness of these and other Arab peoples, the most unambiguous distinctions on TV news were between Egypt and other Arab nations, and between Iran and the rest of the Middle East. Do Americans make such distinctions?

Gallup data do suggest that the American people underwent a corresponding shift toward greater sensitivity to differences among Middle Eastern Moslem nations. For example, Egypt's ranking in 1976, discussed above, was virtually identical with that of Iran, at the time not a very visible country with little TV news attention (48 percent favorable, 37 percent unfavorable, 15 percent don't know). By 1980, while Egypt's scores had soared, Iran's had collapsed to 7 percent favorable, 90 percent unfavorable, 3 percent no opinion. While the 1980 disaffection with Iran is not surprising, the 1976 baseline figures suggest a time when the public perceived no meaningful difference between Egypt and Iran.

There is also evidence that by 1978, the public increasingly distinguished Egypt from other Arab countries. The same Gallup poll asked how likely the respondent thought "a peaceful settlement of differences" would be between Israel and Egypt, and between Israel and "all the Arab nations." The public saw Egypt in different terms from the Arab world in general. The January 1978 survey found that 56 percent thought Israeli peace with Egypt was fairly likely or very likely. However, only 38 percent thought peace with "all the Arab nations" was likely.

A Harris poll in early January 1979 found further distinctions in perceptions of Arab states. Americans were asked if particular countries "really want a just peace in the Middle East." At the top were Egypt and Israel; 52 percent said Egypt really wanted peace compared to 51 percent for Israel. In contrast, 28 percent said Jordan and 26 percent said Saudi Arabia were intent on peace. In the case of both Syria and Libya only 19 percent said they truly wanted peace. At the bottom was the PLO; just 13 percent said the PLO really wanted peace. Americans had been given enough information about the postures of elements in the Middle East that they made clear differentiations.

## Less Favorable Images of Israel?

Content studies in this volume conclude that in the late 1970s, television news coverage became increasingly critical of Israel: Morad Asi found that in 1979, in sharp contrast to previous coverage, a startling plurality of the stories about Israel were unfavorable, and remarkably few were favorable. Itzhak Roeh's examination of the treatment of Israeli activity in southern Lebanon also came to the conclusion that Israel was getting an unfavorable slant. Magda Bagnied and Steven Schneider's comparison of Begin's and Sadat's television personae suggests that Begin suffered in the comparison with Sadat. Jack Shaheen recounts recent network documentaries in which air time is given to people who argue that Israel is the villain in the Middle East.

While most media coverage may have usually been sympathetic to Israel, these findings indicate that an important transition occurred around 1977. If public opinion were responding to TV's more critical approach to Israel, we would expect some decline in Israel's image.

Unlike the first two propositions, however, public opinion did not mirror TV changes toward Israel. Gallup surveys show virtually no change in overall American attitudes toward Israel between 1976 and 1980. In fact, there is an improvement in Israel's overall ratings: the percent favorable to Israel increased from 65 to 74, while the percent unfavorable decreased from 25 to 21. There were no changes at all in the proportion of people who were highly favorable ( + 5, + 4, + 3) toward Israel—31 percent in both years—or in the share of those highly unfavorable ( − 5, − 4, − 3) toward Israel—10 percent in both years.

Israel's popularity remained high despite the changed tenor of TV news coverage. It may be that Israel's general image was sufficiently positive in the United States that it was resistant to relatively short-term fluctuations in its media image.

There may be a further explanation. TV news may have influenced attitudes toward Menachem Begin, toward his administration, or toward selected Israeli policies, without jeopardizing fundamentally sympathetic views toward Isreal. If so, there may be the paradox of continued affection for Israel in the face of a decline in outright allegiance to Israel in the content of its negotiations with Egypt. It is worth noting that, as of January 1980, Egypt's overall approval ranking was only slightly less than that given Israel (71 versus 74 percent positive), and the difference was not statistically significant. Egypt's increased popularity was apparently not at the direct expense of Israel.

The leadership of Israel—rather than the state of Israel—may have suffered the brunt of the more critical coverage. In a revealing Harris poll in April 1978, more Americans said they would trust Israel over Egypt in a disagreement concerning a peace settlement; 43 percent said they would trust Israel and 24 percent said Egypt. However, when asked who they would trust more—President Sadat of Egypt or Prime Minister Begin of Israel—Americans split with 35 percent favoring Sadat and 35 percent saying Begin. The image of Israel's leader had dropped below the level of support for Israel as a whole.

### Increased Recognition of Palestinians

Several of the studies in this volume point to increased television attention to Palestinians and to the PLO. As we noted earlier, the amount of attention given Palestinians relative to that given Israel has increased sharply since 1976. Shaheen reviews some controversial documentaries that added to the visibility of—and perhaps sympathy for—the Palestinians. Bagnied and Schneider observed that in 1977 Sadat frequently discussed the Palestinian issue in a manner that helped to legitimize the topic as a reasonable and important one. Roeh argues that Palestinians were frequently portrayed as helpless, passive victims. Furthermore, Asi shows not only an increase in the amount of coverage given the PLO, but a sharp drop in the amount of negative coverage, with an increase in the proportion of neutral coverage.

These findings would predict that the American public would have become more cognizant of Palestinians and perhaps more amenable to Palestinian claims. A January 1975 Yankelovich survey found that only 52 percent of the public had heard of the PLO. (Gallup did not start including policy questions about the PLO and Palestinians until 1978).

The January 1978 Gallup survey findings are surprising in several respects. To begin with, the proportion of those familiar with the PLO had increased to 77 percent. This represents a rather high level of recognition, although as Table 1.2 shows, the PLO had received fairly large amounts of coverage; with most of the pre-1977 coverage involving terrorism. Of those familiar with the PLO, only 14 percent said the PLO represents the views of most Palestinians. In fact, a big majority, 63 percent, believed that the PLO "does not represent the point of view of a majority of Palestinians;" 23 percent were not sure.

How did so many Americans come to the conclusion the PLO was unrepresentative? It suggests a widespread impression that Palestinians are not as "bad" as the PLO. Yankelovich had found in 1975 that the PLO was strongly viewed as "undemocratic," "anti-American," "backward" "terrorists" (Gruen, 1975). In light of the mostly unfavorable news about the PLO, it is interesting to find that the organization is not equated with Palestinians generally. This distinction may also portend an unexpectedly sympathetic response to Palestinian calls for a homeland.

In January, 1978, Gallup asked respondents who said they followed Middle East news and were aware of the PLO (77 percent of the total sample) whether they favored:

1.   an independent Palestinian nation on the West Bank
2.   a West Bank state affiliated with Jordan
3.   continuation of Palestinians "living as they are now in Israel and in the existing Arab nations."

Some kind of Palestinian state was favored by 46 percent. (A separate Palestinian nation was supported by 24 percent, and one linked to Jordan was supported by 22 percent.) Only 30 percent wanted to continue current arrangements, and 24 percent were undecided.

Subsequent Gallup polls found increased support for an entirely independent Palestinian nation. In May 1978, 32 percent favored separate West Bank status, while 17 percent wanted a state tied to Jordan. The percentage of people wanting to continue the existing situation dropped to 22 percent.

The following year, in March 1979, the Gallup question did not provide the option of a Palestinian state associated with Jordan. Choosing between an entirely independent Palestinian nation or the status quo, 41 percent (of those who follow the Middle East situation) supported establishment of a separate state, while only 28 percent chose the status quo; 31 percent were undecided.

That a plurality of Americans in the Gallup surveys had come to favor a West Bank-Palestinian nation was unexpected, even given increased media attention to the Palestinian people. Americans seem to respond sympathetically to causes that involve the "self-determination" of peoples. Along with an instinctive reaction to favor all "homelands," the survey results are more than consistent with those predicted by television coverage.

## Slight Increase in Overall "Pro-Arab" Opinion

Although the studies in this book detected more favorable treatment of Egypt and less unfavorable treatment of the Palestinians, there was only a little evidence that the rest of the Arab world received more positive coverage. Asi, for example, found little change in the coverage of Syria, Saudi Arabia, Jordan, and Lebanon between 1973 and 1979. Nonetheless, the shift in coverage of Egypt and the Palestinians would still predict somewhat less overall sympathy for Israel.

Gallup has frequently asked the following question to those who "have heard or read about the situation in the Middle East:" "In the Middle East situation, are your sympathies more with Israel or more with the Arab nations?"

In January, 1975, 44 percent said they supported Israel, while only 8 percent supported the Arab nations; the rest had no opinion or favored neither. Through the rest of the 1970s the percentages fluctuated somewhat within a fairly narrow range. By March 1979, the percent favoring the "Arab nations" had increased to 12 percent. Thus, in the dichotomous choice between Israel and the Arabs, a plurality of Americans continued to choose Israel, although Israel's lead fell from a net difference of 36 to 26 percentage points.

A further development was the decline in the proportion of people who said they had no opinion, something to be expected given the media spotlight on the subject. The "no opinion" percentage went from 26 percent in 1975 to 16 percent in 1979. During this same period, the share of the public who were of the opinion that Israel and the Arabs were equally sympathetic (or equally unsympathetic) grew from 22 to 34 percent.

That the actual figures for Israel are not as high as one might suppose is due primarily to two factors: First the absence of any significant pro-Arab bloc of opinion makes the 4-out-of-10 pro-Israeli group appear even larger. Second, pro-Israeli opinion includes a sizable number of articulate, vocal, committed people (Lipset & Schneider, 1977; Lipset, 1978). Coupled with the favorable coverage of Israel, these two factors have helped make public opinion seem to be more overwhelmingly and solidly pro-Israel than has been the case.

The overall modest decline in support for Israel is consistent with what would have been expected if public opinion were responding to television coverage. A different result might have emerged had the survey asked a comparison of Israel with Egypt, but on the omnibus Israel vs. Arabs question, Israel continues to hold a decided plurality.

In a series of four surveys in 1978 and 1979, Gallup asked those who followed Middle Eastern news: "Do you think Israel is or is not doing all it should do to bring about peace in the Middle East?" The identical question was posed for Egypt. In each of these surveys—by small margins—Americans were more likely to say that Egypt was doing what it should do for peace than was Israel.

In the last poll in March, 1979, 90 percent of the total sample said they were aware of the situation in the Middle East. Of that group, 36 percent said Egypt was doing what it should for peace in contrast to 28 percent willing to say the same thing for Israel. Conversely, 43 percent said Egypt. was not doing enough for peace, while 51 percent said Israel was not.

Once again the public opinion data coincide with the media findings of a more critical posture toward Israel and an increasingly receptive view of Egypt. However, the crucial caveat is that TV news and public opinion evidenced only a slight trend toward a more positive image of Arab nations in general or toward the "Arab side" in fundamental conflicts with Israel, despite the wish for a Palestinian "homeland."

### Spurious Correlations?

Four of the five general trends in television news content coincided with parallel trends in American public opinion. The one TV trend that did not show a simple corresponding opinion change—regarding the overall image of Israel—did however coincide with more specific changes in opinions, such as disillusionment with Israel's commitment to working for peace. Correlations alone are not sufficient to "prove" that television news was the chief cause of the shifts in public opinion. Newspapers and news magazines might have had similar content changes and could have been a more important factor. Americans may also have been reacting to signals from the Carter administration in the direction of greater support for Egypt and more concern with Palestinians.

The set of correlations does prompt us to invoke that favorite phrase for provocative but less than definite evidence—"highly suggestive." It is highly suggestive that public opinion on the Middle East should fit so closely the trends in television news. After all, information about foreign events—unlike domestic topics, such as inflation—is almost entirely derived from the media. Our findings are consistent with the idea that attitudes toward international affairs are especially influenced by television news content.

While television news over most of the 1970s concentrated on the Arab-Israeli conflict, as noted previously, coverage changed enormously with the Soviet occupation of Afghanistan and the hostage crisis in Iran. The final two sections of this chapter examine coverage of these subjects.

## DISCOVERING AFGHANISTAN

"Afghanistan" used to have a special meaning for journalists. As a remote, backward country, it represented exactly the sort of topic that most mass-market news outlets could not afford to cover. Only the *New York Times* was believed capable of periodically updating Americans on so esoteric a topic as Afghanistan. Perhaps if the Kabul government presided over oil, or if the US had a few million Afghan-Americans, the country's news value would be greater; instead, Afghanistan was well-chosen as a symbol for nations that only the *Times* might care about.

As a result, it came as no shock when our data showed the usual absence of any TV news involving Afghanistan during most of the 1970s. The 1972–1978 coverage of the country was so brief it can be recounted easily.

Afghanistan was not on network news at all during 1972. Each network ran one story in 1973 when Lt. General Muhammed Daud came to power in a "bloodless coup"—a total of about 60 seconds on ABC, 40 seconds on CBS, and 10 seconds on NBC. We were unable to find a single story on Afghanistan on any of the weeknight network newscasts in 1974, 1975, 1976, and 1977.

Daud was arrested in 1978 and later killed in the "Great Saur Revolution." Afghanistan was renamed the "Democratic Republic of Afghanistan" and the sole legal party became the "People's Democratic Party of Afghanistan." These and other pivotal developments in Afghanistan were largely ignored by the networks: During the entire year, NBC had two brief stories which totalled less than half a minute. ABC and CBS had only slightly more coverage; the 5 brief stories on ABC came to less than 3 minutes total, and the 3 on CBS lasted less than 2 minutes altogether. Allowing for a certain amount of inertia, the reaction may have been that a new Democratic Republic of Afghanistan was not much more newsworthy than the old obscure neutralist Afghanistan.

More unexpected was the perfunctory coverage that was given the subsequent February 1979 kidnapping and assassination of American Ambassador Dubs. Weeknight coverage of his murder added up to only 2½ minutes on NBC, 5 minutes on ABC, and 8 minutes on CBS. We could find no follow-up to the story the next month.

The murder of Dubs might have been a warning flag of plots and up-heaval in Kabul, but again Afghanistan dropped off the network agenda. (Treatment of the death of this US diplomat also contrasts wildly with treatment of the incarceration of US diplomats in Tehran.)

In the meantime, off-camera, the People's Democratic Party government was torn by factions, the party and army were purged, and party leaders changed. Headline writers would note "cabals in Kabul." The Soviets became progressively more entangled with the problems of the ruling regime, and on December 25–26, 1979, started airlifting troops to Kabul. By December 27, Hafizullah Amin was overthrown and executed while a more "dependable" government, lead by Babrak Karmal, was installed by the Soviets. The leader of the Israeli Labor Party, Shimon Peres said (1980, p. 888): "For the first time since World War II, the Red Army has been sent in to conquer a country which is outside the recognized Soviet orbit—surely a source of concern to the other countries neighboring the U.S.S.R." President Jimmy Carter called it the biggest crisis since World War II.

The initial radical, pro-Soviet putsch had not been enough, nor had the murder of the US Ambassador, but the physical occupation of Kabul by Soviet troops finally made Afghanistan highly newsworthy. At last the symbol of obscurity had the full attention of the media, and, for that matter, the White House. The occupation of Afghanistan became one of the six major TV news stories about the Middle East in the 1972–80 period, along with the 1973 war and oil embargo, the trip of Sadat to Jerusalem, the Camp David Summit, the fall of the Shah, and US hostages in Iran.

Geographical purists will contend that Afghanistan should not be labeled as part of the Middle East, that it is actually in southwest or south-central Asia. In shaping the way we think about the world, however, television news firmly planted Afghanistan in the Middle East region. Backdrop maps emphasized Afghanistan's proximity to the Persian Gulf rather than the Himalayas. The nation's geopolitical significance, as far as TV news was concerned, came from its being adjacent to Iran, not Pakistan, and came from its "proximity" to key oil fields.

David Paletz and Roberta Pearson (1978, pp. 78–80) have identified a practice they term news "clustering." The networks, they observed, package a set of stories together in a segment. Each "cluster" would have added coherence by having the same anchor, perhaps a similar backdrop, and a similar general theme, such as the economy or Western European affairs. Afghanistan became part of the Middle East-turmoil cluster, often accompanied by news of Iran.

NBC again had the least amount of coverage with 71 stories about Afghanistan in 1980; ABC again had the most coverage with 112 stories, and CBS had 93 stories. On all three networks, coverage was greatest during the first quarter of 1980 and then dropped sharply.

Montague Kern, in a study published in this volume, has analyzed the use of sources in reporting the Afghan story. Her finding regarding network reliance on the State Department is consistent with the pattern of attention given the country by TV news. The salience of the story for Carter's State Department coincided with its prominence on the networks. Prior to the airlift of Soviet troops neither the networks nor State had much to say publicly about the activities in Afghanistan.

The correlation by itself does not indicate which, if either, was the independent variable; it does confirm the notion that meaningful attention by either the networks or the State Department stimulates and may insure more attention by the other. (Compare coverage of pre-invasion Afghanistan with that of Poland, for example.)

The case of Afghanistan provides further evidence for the screen against bilateral third-party news, as set forth earlier. Short of violence and State Department activity, Soviet-Afghan relations were not very newsworthy. Even after Dubs' death, the presumption of Afghanistan's unnewsworthiness was not overcome until Soviet troops finally showed up in force.

## IRAN: TV's DAY ONE THRU DAY 444

In a provocative essay in this volume, David Altheide explores in detail the nature of coverage during the first six months of the hostage crisis. Chapter 8 is the first report of his broader study of media coverage of Iran and represents an important systematic assessment of the content of a very large sample of stories. To help put Altheide's study in perspective and to consider some broader issues, it is important to understand just how intensively Iran was covered and to examine why it was covered so much.

No other episode in recent history has dominated TV news quite like the story of American hostages in Tehran. Night after night for over fourteen months, the networks spotlighted chanting Iranian mobs, cautious US spokesmen, stoic hostage families, sundry international courts and commissions, candles and yellow ribbons, staged tapes of hostages, insistent Iranian spokesmen, Christmas and Easter with the hostages, a failed rescue attempt, swaggering militants, presidential campaign implications, negotiation rumors and endless speculation. After the Inaugural hour release, the story climaxed with coverage of a succession of homecomings—in Wiesbaden, in West Point, in Washington, in New York, in hometowns, and, finally, in neighborhoods.

Ironically, one of the first activities of the freed Americans in Wiesbaden was to watch a review of news on the medium they had so thoroughly dominated for the preceeding 14½ months. The State Department had asked Fay Schreibman and one of the authors, William Adams, to prepare a videotape anthology of several hours of TV news highlights to update the released hostages. (See Agus, 1981; Van Riper, 1981.) To help fill their informational vacuum, the 5½ hours of tapes included network news stories about a wide range of subjects. Reflecting the networks' priorities, however, a majority of the stories concerned the two topics that had overshadowed all else on TV news—the presidential campaign and the hostage crisis itself.

At the White House, former charge d'affaires Bruce Laingen turned to President Reagan and said, referring to their US welcome, "I hope you were watching TV" in order to appreciate it. Indeed, television was the crucial medium for appreciating the significance and impact of this crisis.

The sheer volume of television coverage was extraordinary. For the first six months of the hostage captivity, the networks devoted nearly one-third of each weeknight newscast to the story. During most six-month periods between 1965 and 1975, even the war in Vietnam was not given as much coverage.

## Iran as the Big Story

Objectively the crisis in Iran and the war in Vietnam had little in common, other than that the United States was "tied down" for some time by its link to both. Yet, as objects of news coverage, Iran and Vietnam had several features in common. Iran became a "television crisis" in some of the same respects that Vietnam became a "television war." In the 1960s for the first time Americans watched the seven o'clock news in their living rooms and witnessed US soldiers fighting and dying the Southeast Asia. Some of that same tragic intimacy was repeated with Iran. Americans viewed the bodies of the servicemen from the failed rescue mission, saw the weary and sad families of the hostages and other equally emotional sights.

Like Vietnam, Iran became the continuing international crisis that displaced all others in their claims for television air time. Iran became a stock element in the nightly news, often despite the absence of any tangible developments. The number of days Americans were held captive even became incorporated into Walter Cronkite's "and-that's-the-way-it-is" sign-off. While a number of international stories have been given saturation coverage confined to a few weeks (e.g., Camp David Summit, Sadat's trip to Jerusalem), only Vietnam and Iran are rivals for extensive coverage over a period of many months.

If the first six months of the hostage story are used as the basis for comparison, then nightly coverage of Iran appears to have surpassed average nightly coverage of Vietnam (except perhaps during 1968), using the figures reported by Frank (1973) for 1972 or extrapolating from Bailey's data (1976) for the 1965–70 period.

If the first twelve months of the hostage story are used for comparison (November 1979–October 1980) then attention that was given Iran still matches or exceeds the total annual coverage of the Vietnam war in several years. At the start of 1972 over 150,000 American troops were in Vietnam; all Vietnam news on CBS that year totalled 1092 minutes (Lefever, 1974, p. 26). In the first twelve months that the 53 American hostages were in Iran, CBS devoted 1026 minutes to their story.

Don Oberdorfer (1979, 1981) has argued that, thanks to this saturation media coverage, the hostage crisis, like the Tet offensive in Vietnam, will prove to have been a watershed "Big Event" that fundamentally molded the public's worldview. It might be added that unlike Vietnam, the justness of the US role with regard to Iran was clearly endorsed by the networks.

Most academic studies concluded that TV news treatment of Southeast Asia was either hostile to the US role (e.g., Lefever,1974; Herz, 1980) or was "balanced" by giving about equal time to themes of opposition and support of US involvement (e.g., Russo, 1971; Pride & Wamsley, 1972). In coverage of Iran, however, Ramsey Clark did not replace J. William Fulbright. In fact, the evidence compiled by Altheide, as well as the impressions of other observers (Shales, 1980; Said, 1980), indicates that Iranian coverage overwhelmingly presumed the righteousness of the American position and supported the plodding but persistent approach of the Carter administration.

In any case, Oberdorfer is clearly justified in adding Iran to his list of television's Big Events. To measure the precise dimensions of the coverage, we tabulated all of the weekday, early evening network news stories about the hostages as recorded in Vanderbilt University's *Television News Index and Abstracts*. Our tally is a conservative one because we only included stories that were explicitly tied to the US hostages. Consequently, we excluded such stories as the Iranian embassy takeovers in Paris and London, the DC-10 crashing in Iran, and the increase in illegal drugs from Iran since the revolution. We even excluded some stories that had a strong implicit connection to the general crisis—for example, some stories about anti-Shah demonstrations that lacked an explicit link to the hostages, and stories about the Shah's health and travels that were not directly incorporated into hostage-related accounts. Even using this rather strict definition of the hostage story, by television standards the volume of coverage was colossal.

Table 1.3 presents the monthly totals for each network until the end of 1980. ABC provided the most coverage, with an average of almost seven minutes every weeknight for the first six months. NBC invariably gave less coverage to the story than either ABC (which led 8 months) or CBS (which led 6 months). These differences seem consistent with the notions that *ABC's World News Tonight*, with a European-based anchor, tried to offer slightly more worldwide news than the competition; that ABC—along with introducing its new late-night *America Held Hostage* show—sought to identify itself as the key source for Iranian news; that NBC's nightly "Special Segment" had a domestic focus and reduced the remaining air time for hostage stories; and that NBC continued its pattern since 1976 of airing less Middle East news than the other networks. Yet, even NBC's coverage of the hostage story was considerable for TV news, and Table 1.3 is probably more notable for the similarities rather than the differences among the networks.

In November and December of 1979, the hostage story consumed about half of the average weeknight newscast on ABC and CBS. (Recall that an early evening network news program usually has between 22 and 23 actual minutes of news time, after subtracting commercials and closing credits.) The networks immediately pitched the story at the very top of the news agenda and kept it there night after night. In sharp contrast to coverage of the seizure of the *Pueblo,* the takeover of the US Embassy in Tehran remained at the highest visibility. After a flurry of news, the *Pueblo* had reverted to obscurity during the ensuing weeks of behind-the-scenes negotiations.

Coverage did drop after the networks were expelled from Iran in mid-January (see Weinraub, 1980). Throughout the remainder of the winter and into the spring, however, coverage stayed at very high levels, averaging around 4 minutes of news time each weeknight in the January–April period. Sustained coverage continued despite the formal start of the presidential campaign.

Table 1.3
Coverage of the Hostage Crisis on Network News

| | ABC | | CBS | | NBC | |
|---|---|---|---|---|---|---|
| | \multicolumn{6}{l}{Average Number of Minutes about the Hostage Story on Weeknight News Programs (Total minutes per month in parentheses)} | | | | | |
| 1979: | | | | | | |
| November | 12.1 | (242.3) | 11.4 | (227.0) | 9.9 | (198.3) |
| December | 11.1 | (233.6) | 10.0 | (210.7) | 7.8 | (156.5) |
| 1980: | | | | | | |
| January | 4.3 | (99.8) | 3.7 | (84.3) | 3.5 | (78.0) |
| February | 4.4 | (92.7) | 3.8 | (80.0) | 3.4 | (70.6) |
| March | 3.1 | (64.2) | 3.1 | (65.0) | 2.8 | (58.2) |
| April | 6.6 | (146.3) | 6.8 | (150.2) | 5.9 | (129.7) |
| May | 2.5 | (55.0) | 2.0 | (43.8) | .8 | (17.5) |
| June | 1.1 | (23.2) | 1.4 | (29.2) | .7 | (14.6) |
| July | 1.7 | (38.3) | 1.4 | (33.0) | .8 | (18.8) |
| August | 1.1 | (23.0) | .9 | (18.5) | .6 | (12.0) |
| September | 1.5 | (32.2) | 1.1 | (25.1) | 1.1 | (24.0) |
| October | 2.1 | (49.4) | 2.6 | (59.0) | 1.8 | (41.5) |
| November | 3.1 | (61.9) | 3.2 | (63.2) | 1.8 | (35.8) |
| December | 3.8 | (87.4) | 4.3 | (99.3) | 3.2 | (73.0) |
| First 6 month av. | 6.9 minutes | | 6.4 minutes | | 5.5 minutes | |
| OVERALL AVERAGE | 4.1 minutes | | 3.9 minutes | | 3.1 minutes | |

TV news is famous for its devotion to presidential campaigns (Epstein, 1973; Robinson, 1977), especially the early primaries. It is not unusual for the presidential campaign to be given one-quarter of all news time each leap year (e.g., Lefever, 1974, p. 26). During the months when the primaries began, Soviet troops moved into Afghanistan, but neither the invasion nor the campaign dislodged Iran.

Finally in May, 1980, coverage dropped off sharply. After the failed rescue attempt, miscellaneous international emissaries, and relentlessly disappointing optimistic rumors, coverage fell back to an average of around one or two minutes a newscast throughout the summer and into early autumn. This coverage appeared almost inattentive in contrast to the onslaught of the first six months, and some people voiced concern that "America might forget about the hostages." Again, however, by the norms of television—especially for what was by the summer a fairly "steady-state" story—"vigil journalism" continued at a high pace.

From mid-October through the end of the year, coverage reverted to higher levels with the increasingly visible negotiations. The hostages flew from Tehran to freedom on January 20th and were given virtually equal billing with the installation of a radically-different US president (Diamond, 1981; Kaiser, 1981; Shales, 1981).

One could construct a long list of ratios to contrast the time spent on the hostages with the time given a variety of other topics over the past decade. The amount of Iranian coverage was so great that such ratios would further dramatize the daily blitz of Iranian news. We think it suffices to point out that only Vietnam, Watergate, and presidential campaigns were in the same league with the hostage story in terms of heavy, long-term coverage.

With such data, it also becomes easy to argue on a coldly logical basis that coverage of Iran was excessive and that any number of other developments were intrinsically more consequential for the United States. This makes it all the more important to try to understand why the hostage story garnered such a huge volume of coverage.

### The TV News Appeal of Iran

Why did news gravitate so strongly toward the hostage story? What factors help explain its extraordinary volume of attention? We propose six elements that, added together, can account for the extended coverage:

1. the traditional newsworthiness formula
2. human interest and humanitarian concern
3. television drama
4. Iranian accessibility
5. Presidential priorities
6. symbolic appeal

By any traditional standard, the Embassy takeover and the holding of US diplomats were of course "newsworthy." The events constituted change from the status quo, were highly unusual, and were relevant to a wide audience. Although the conventional news value of the story does explain why it earned some attention, it is not sufficient to explain the magnitude of attention it received. Additional factors helped catapult it to greater prominence.

No one would deny, for example, that there was sincere concern for the fate of the hostages. The fear that lives were at stake fueled the perceived newsworthiness of the story. The network response to a "human interest angle" was no surprise, and worked to reinforce humanitarian concern for their plight.

These two initial factors became explosive when they combined with a third powerful factor—Iran offered phenomenal TV news drama. Edward Epstein's classic *News From Nowhere* (1973) described the ingredients that made an ordinary news story highly desirable for TV news, and the hostage story turned out to be overflowing with each of these TV attractions.

Epstein found that, in order to attract an audience and maintain their ratings, network news people looked for dramatic, conflictual stories, of interest to the entire nation, that could be vividly shown with "good pictures" and action footage, and that had "easily recognizable" images, simple themes, and plot with two opposing sides; stories had added appeal if the president was involved and if there was some predictability of locales and sources. Using these criteria, it is difficult to conceive of a story more ideally suited to the demands of TV news than the hostage crisis.

Since various technological advances had removed most of the limitations on instantaneous coverage of such a distant drama, Iran had it all: straightforward and fundamental conflict between two sides; a powerful elementary theme (what is or will be happening to the American hostages?); good footage of worried families, the earnest President, the bearded Ayatollah, and even sometimes-blindfolded hostages themselves; action pictures of angry crowds in Iran and in the United States; adding up to a continuing, suspenseful, telegenic narrative of nationwide appeal.

Closely linked with its TV appeal is the fourth factor shaping the magnitude of coverage—Iranian accessibility. Consider the weakened cumulative impact of the story if, from the very beginning, all Western correspondents had been barred from Iran, leaders in Iran had refused interviews and had pursued their claims through non-dramatic diplomatic channels rather than television channels. Instead, both the city of Tehran and the leaders of Iran were, under the circumstances, astonishingly open to American and other Western media.

Apparently, Iranians anticipated that media exposure would persuade Americans of the virtues of their cause (see Mather, 1979; Shales, 1979; Hanauer, 1979; Randal, 1979; Griffith, 1979). Iranian leaders rivaled Hodding Carter at the State Department in answering media questions.

Even after US cameras and correspondents were ousted—and the size of the crowds around the US embassy immediately dropped—pictures and stories were still available from European sources. The point here is not that Iran manipulated the networks to portray them sympathetically, although it was clearly attempted. Our point is that by providing so much access—in the hope it would rebound to their favor—Iran did bolster the story's visibility on television news.

Back in the United States, the story's visibility profited from President Carter's involvement. As Epstein (1973), Grossman and Kumar (1981), and others have observed, television news is quite sensitive to the agenda and activities of the president. At the same time, these dynamics are interactive. While the media may respond to the president, the president also responds to the media. It is awkward for the president to be shown ignoring a conflict that Cronkite, Chancellor, and Reynolds all agreed was the most significant news of the day. Nonetheless, intense Presidential activities on behalf of the hostages (even if triggered in part by the network agenda) further heightened the story's priority on the network agenda.

The story of the Americans held in Tehran became more than just news with high Presidential involvement and human interest and good pictures. It became imbued with immense symbolic significance. Commentators have made much of television's attraction to events that seem to be a "microcosm" and seem to represent and symbolize larger phenomena (e.g., Braestrup, 1978), and, at the same time, political actors themselves often concentrate on the level of symbols and evocative gestures.

In the case of the hostages in Iran, the symbolism was multi-faceted and helps explain why the entire episode resonated so strongly and instinctively with Americans, including people in the news media. The frustrations of the last two decades of US foreign policy seemed epitomized: An American sanctuary is overrun by a people embittered by what were supposed to have been the ultimately benevolent purposes of past US support. American diplomats, and by association part of the nation itself, are incarcerated by people with seemingly incomprehensible, irrational, or sinister motivations. Reluctant to be a bully or a coward, the US Government tries to be firm yet conciliatory, strong but unabrasive, to speak calmly and carry a yellow ribbon.

Iran crystallized the dilemmas and anger associated with such fundamental issues as how to exercise American power effectively, the sense of impotence in world affairs after a string of defeats, how to communicate with seemingly mad and unstable peoples and regimes, the sham and pretense of international forums, the pernicious moves of the Soviets, and how to deal with renegade states without being bellicose.

Such themes pervaded coverage of the hostage crisis with unusual clarity because they were not drowned out by American *mea culpae*. Iranians had managed to construct an incident so egregious, inappropriate, and

aggressive, that the malevolence of the Shah was immaterial and any past
US culpability was irrelevent. The liberal *New Republic* was so incensed at
even the minor amount of apologetic press that they editorialized (1981, p. 7):

> For more than a year, journalists, clerics, and professors have been
> dishing up the usual anthropological abracadabra about the different
> ways and different values of the Iranians...[i.e.,] *Tout comprendre*
> *c'est tout pardonner*. In the end, it turns out, grasping the motives of
> the mullahs requires no course in Persian anthropology. Deceitful they
> are, and cruel too—but not so strange to a world that has known other
> mad rulers. For what, after all the posturing and talk of holy men,
> does it take to win the release of our hostages? Money, lots of it. That is
> something we can understand. And it is something that should provoke
> nothing so much as disgust. Any appropriate policy toward Iran must
> begin with this feeling of revulsion.

Having provoked revulsion, Iran provided a story that could be—
and, Altheide has found, was—portrayed unambiguously with the United
States as the aggrieved and virtuous party. In a context free from the usual
fear of "another Vietnam," the hostage story could be portrayed as a
unified, just nation determined to free countrymen caught in another painful eruption of foreign barbarism.

The skeptic can always return to compare the number of hostages in
Tehran with, for example, the number of daily traffic fatalities in the US,
the number of dissidents in the Gulag, the number of starving Cambodians
or the number of massacred Christians in Chad—all recently involving a
greater potential and actual loss of life than the Embassy takeover. (On
coverage of Cambodia, see Adams & Joblove, 1980.) To be sure, such
tragedies can also be embodied with strong symbols. The hostage story,
however, merged its awesome symbolism and clear-cut themes with Iranian accessibility, Presidential participation, national implications, and
elements made-to-order for the dramaturgy of television news.

## Some Repercussions of Televised Terrorism

Measuring the independent impact of media messages is never easy,
least of all in a complex crisis. Distinguishing the separate contribution of
television news from the rest of the media is even more difficult. Nonetheless, we believe a few reasoned speculations are in order.

To begin with, it is clear that political elites both in the United States
and in Iran were extremely concerned about broadcast coverage of events
from the very start of the crisis. President Carter let it be known that he
considered the early treatment of confrontations between marching Iranian
students and angry Americans to be inflammatory and dangerous. A few
weeks later, State Department spokesman Hodding Carter, in an "off-the-
record" talk, complained that the networks were manipulated by the

shrewd Iranians (Carmody 1979). Throughout the crisis, the Administration was careful to articulate its position, frequently and on camera.

Similar concern with US television was evident in Iran. Signs outside the embassy were quickly painted in English and aimed at the cameras. Iranian students in the United States phoned home daily to explain how events in Iran were being depicted by the networks. At one point, NBC even broadcast a contrived television interview with a hostage including unedited monologues by Iranian militants. In late November, Khomeini's media advisors granted interview time ranked according to the ratings, giving CBS the longest session and relegating PBS to a distant fourth priority. When US newspeople were eventually viewed as counterproductive, they were quickly thrown out of Iran. Moreover, interviews with Iranian officials also revealed sensitivity to how unfolding events were portrayed on US television. The militants equipped the embassy itself with cameras, a microwave dish, and transmitters to feed film to the main TV station. Iranians clearly wanted "good TV stories" (Mather, 1979; Schardt, 1979; Randal, 1979; Shales, 1979; Griffith, 1979; Weinraub, 1980; "Tehran's Reluctant Diplomats," 1979).

Due to American influence on international communication, the US news media agenda has an impact on the play of news worldwide. All the evidence indicates that key individuals on both sides were worried about TV images and impressions on America and on the world. That in itself does not mean that they would have acted differently in the absence of such intense coverage, but if coverage had been low key, one must ask:

Would low-key coverage have made it easier for the Iranians to back down, save face, and release the hostages sooner? Would low-key coverage have diminished the thrill of, as one Iranian negotiator was widely quoted as saying, rubbing "the nose of the biggest superpower in the world in the dust"? Would low-key coverage have persuaded Iranians sooner that they would never get enough unedited air time to convince the US public to return the Shah and meet other demands? Would low-key coverage have made it politically easier for Carter to accede to some Iranian demands? Would the President, Secretary of State, and others have moved more quickly to upgrade other international concerns? The logical answer to all of these questions is "yes." Yet, because so little in the hostage crisis was predictable or "logical"—from Day 1 through Day 444—such logical conclusions are the sheerest speculation.

In a prescient front-page story in the *Washington Post*, just three weeks after the embassy takeover, Don Oberdorfer wrote that "there is growing evidence the long-running crisis may be one of those rare international 'hinge events' that change the way people think and governments act, therefore altering the course of history." Oberdorfer noted the impact of television's transmission of the "shocking symbols and well as substance into the living rooms of the American people," and how all other diplomatic priorities of the US government had quickly "been subordinated to the plight of the hostages." Oberdorfer said that at the start of the crisis "three weeks of soaring tension seemed inconceivable." "Three more weeks or even more seems an almost intolerable prospect today," he wrote nearly 14 months before the Americans were released.

As a very long-running "hinge event" that could "change the way people think," the hostage story suggested a couple of key themes: Despite several years of trying to placate the Third World and the Soviets (1) it's a menacing world out there and (2) it may be better confronted through strength than sentimentality. Then 1980 brought a succession of events to reinforce these themes, starting off with Soviet troops overrunning Afghanistan and punctuated by disturbing reports of Soviet military might, by President Carter's newfound mistrust of the USSR, by upheaval in Poland, and by guerillas in Central America.

In precisely this same period, survey researchers recorded the largest change in the spending priorities of Americans since their polls had begun. The proportion of Americans who thought the government should spend more on defense more than doubled, increasing from 26 percent in 1978 to 60 percent in 1980 ("Opinion Roundup," 1980). We will not be surprised if future data analysis shows the change was greatest among television-reliant citizens. The indispensible element for this change was surely the high-level media visibility and portrayal of certain key events.

The hostage story was the supernova in a constellation of foreign stories that were shown nightly and illuminated a new perspective. Had diplomats in Tehran been treated more like the crew of the Pueblo, had Poland in 1980 been covered more like Czechoslovakia in 1968, had the fall of Afghanistan been depicted more like the fall of Cambodia, had Central America been portrayed more like south-central Africa two years before, and had the build-up of Soviet military hardware in 1980 been ignored as it had been in the early 1970s, we doubt that Ronald Reagan's campaign rhetoric would have been sufficient to stimulate the massive swing in public opinion. Rather, it was necessary that such events be center stage, or center screen, and be shown as ultimately "menacing," rather than merely "unfortunate."

A final implication of the hostage story is associated with concepts that students of political socialization refer to as "diffuse support," "system legitimation," and "transmission and maintenance of positive societal affect" in other words, having a sense of unity, loyalty, and attachment toward the country. The large volume of coverage of the hostage story coupled with its sometimes thinly-disguised chauvanism provided an occasion for an outpouring of collective outrage, frustration, and finally euphoria.

With so many centrifugal forces operating to rupture social cohesion, the solidarity evoked by the hostage crisis is a potent force. One returning Marine, whose first political memories as a young American must have begun with the bitterness of Vietnam and Watergate, was so stunned by the tens of thousands of joyous flag-waving young people, old people, and cross-section of Americans that he tearfully said, "I'd go through it all over again if I had to—it was actually worth it—just to see the country so unified."

## FUTURE MIDDLE EAST COVERAGE

Coverage of Iran and Afghanistan was a mammoth aberation in the sweep of the past decade of Middle East news. It seems likely that the Arab-Israeli conflict will be reasserted as the prominent "issue" in the region. If the pattern of the past continues, news such as the Yemens' war, Kaddifi's activities, and other stories from north Africa, the Arabian peninsula, and states distant from Israel, as well as the independent moves of the Soviet Union, European countries, and the United Nations, will be given relatively little news time.

Arab and Israeli leaders will surely continue to be concerned about how they appear to the American television audience. As Prime Minister Begin observed (Friedman, 1980, p. 83), "In our times, you have to talk indeed not only to governments but to public opinion." And, in fact, on issues between the Arabs and Israel, US public opinion did appear to be correlated with television news coverage. Future television news coverage of the Middle East will be "worth watching" for a variety of important reasons.

## REFERENCES

Adams, William C. 1978. Network News Research in Perspective: A Bibliographic Essay. In William Adams and Fay Schreibman, eds., *Television Network News: Issues in Content Research*. Washington, D.C.: School of Public and International Affairs, George Washington University, pp. 11–46.

————, 1981. *Television Coverage of International Affairs*. Norwood, N.J.: Ablex.

———— and Paul H. Ferber. 1977. Television Interview Shows: The Politics of Visibility. *Journal of Broadcasting* 21 (Spring): 141–151.

———— and Michael Joblove. 1980. The Unnewsworthy Holocaust. *Policy Review* 11 (Winter): 59–67.

———— and Suzanne Albin. 1980. Public Information on Social Change: Television Coverage of Women in the Workforce. *Policy Studies Journal* 8 (Spring): 717–734.

Agus, Carole. 1981. Catching Up to the Present. *Newsday*, January 24, 1981.

Bailey, George. 1976. Television War: Trends in Network Coverage of Vietnam, 1965–1970. *Journal of Broadcasting* 20 (Spring): 147–158.

Batscha, Robert M. 1975. *Foreign Affairs News and the Broadcast Journalist*. New York: Praeger.

Belkaoui, Janice Monti. 1978. Images of Arabs and Israelis in the Prestige Press, 1966–1974. *Journalism Quarterly* 55 (Winter): 732–738.

Benjamin, Milton. 1975. The Other Battlefield. *Newsweek* (April 4, 1975): 52–53.

Braestrup, Peter. 1978. *Big Story*. Garden City, N.Y.: Anchor Books.

Carmody, John. 1979. TV Column: Networks Fight Back! *Washington Post*, December 7, 1979.

Comstock, George; Steven Chaffee; Natan Katzman; Maxwell McCombs; and Donald Roberts. 1978. *Television and Human Behavior*. New York: Columbia University Press.

Darling, Lynn. 1980. The Gray Ghost of Crisis. *Washington Post*, February 7, 1980.

Diamond, Edwin. 1981. The Day TV News Brought Us Together. *Panorama* (April): 31–33ff.

Epstein, Edward J. 1973. *News From Nowhere*. New York: Random House.

Erskine, Hazel. 1969. The Polls: Western Partisanship in the Middle East. *Public Opinion Quarterly* 33 (Winter 1969–70): 627–640.

Feith, Douglas J. 1980. Israel, the *Post*, and the Shaft. *Middle East Review* 12 (Summer): 62–66.

Frank, Robert S. 1973. *Message Dimensions of Television News*. Lexington, Mass.: Lexington Books.

Friedman, Jane. 1980. Has TV Tilted Against Israel? *Panorama* (December): 40–43ff.

Gans, Herbert J. 1979. *Deciding What's News*. New York: Pantheon Books.

Griffith, Thomas. 1979. The 'Self-Restraint' Brownout. *Time* 114 (December 17, 1979): 106.

Gerbner, George and George Marvanyi. 1977. The Many World's of the Press. *Journal of Communication* 27 (Winter 1977): 52–66.

Gordon, Avishag H. 1975. The Middle East October 1973 War as Reported by the American Networks. *International Problems* 14 (Fall 1975): 76–85.

Graber, Doris. 1980. *Mass Media and American Politics*. Washington, D.C.: Congressional Quarterly Press.

Grossman, Michael B. and Martha J. Kumar. 1981. *Portraying the President*. Baltimore, Md.: Johns Hopkins University Press.

Gruen, George E. 1975. Arab Petropower and American Public Opinion. *Middle East Review* 7 (Winter 1975–76): 33–39.

Hadar, Leon T. 1980. Behind *The New York Times* Middle East Coverage. *Middle East Review* 12 (Summer 1980): 56–61.

Hanauer, Joan. 1979. Ayatollah Uses Television the American Way. *Dallas Morning News*, December 19, 1979.

Heikal, Mohomed. 1978. *The Sphinx and the Commisar*. New York: Harper and Row.

Herz, Martin. 1980. *The Prestige Press and the Christmas Bombing, 1972*. Washington, D.C.: Ethics and Public Policy Center.

Ibrahim, Saad. 1974. American Domestic Forces and the October War. *Journal of Palestine Studies* 4 (Autumn 1974): 55–81.

Interviews: American Media and the Palestine Problem. 1976. *Journal of Palestine Studies* 5 (Fall-Winter 1976): 127–149.

Kaiser, Robert G. 1981. America's 'Great Adhesive' Serves Up a Pageant and a Thriller. *Washington Post*, January 21, 1981.

Kohut, Andrew. 1978. American Opinion on Shifting Sands. *Public Opinion* 1 (May/June 1978): 15–18.

Kraus, Sidney; Dennis Davis; Gladys Engel Lang; Kurt Lang. Critical Events Analysis. 1975. In Steven H. Chaffee, ed., *Political Communication: Issues and Strategies for Research*. Beverly Hills, Ca.: Sage.

Larson, James. 1979. International Affairs Coverage on U.S. Network Television. *Journal of Communication* 29 (Spring 1979): 136–147.

Lefever, Ernest W. 1974. *TV and National Defense*. Boston, Va.: Institute for American Strategy.

Leebron, Elizabeth J. 1978. An Analysis of Selected United States Media Coverage of the 1972 Munich Olympic Tragedy. Ph.D. dissertation. Northwestern University.

Lent, John. 1977. Foreign News in American Media. *Journal of Communication* 27 (Winter 1977): 46–51.

Lipset, Seymour Martin. 1978. Further Commentary on American Attitudes. *Public Opinion* 1 (May/June 1978): 16–17.

——— and William Schneider. 1977. Carter vs. Israel: What the Polls Reveal. *Commentary* 64 (November 1977): 21–29.

Mather, Ian. 1979. In Tehran, Crowds Find Media for Their Message. *Washington Star*, November 16, 1979.

Mishra, V. M. 1979. News from the Middle East in Five U.S. Media. *Journalism Quarterly* 56 (Summer 1979): 374–378.

Mosettig, Michael and Henry Griggs, Jr. 1980. TV at the Front. *Foreign Policy* 38 (Spring 1980); 67–79.

*New Republic* editorial. 1981. Not One Cent for Tribute. *New Republic* 184 (January 3, 1981): 5–7.

Oberdorfer, Don. 1979. Iran: Rare "Hinge Event." *Washington Post*, November 25, 1979.

———· 1981. Hostage Seizure: Enormous Consequences. *Washington Post*, January 23, 1981.

———· 1981. Why the Hostage Crisis Held Us All Hostage. *Washington Post*, February 1, 1981.

Opinion Roundup. 1980. *Public Opinion* 3 (October/November 1980): 22–26.

Padelford, Edward A. 1979. The Regional American Press: An Analysis of Its Reporting and Commentary on the Arab-Israeli Situation. Ph.D. dissertation, American University.

Paletz, David and Roberta Pearson. 1978. "The Way You Look Tonight": A Critique of Television News Criticism. In William Adams and Fay Schreibman, eds., *Television Network News: Issues in Content Research*. Washington, D.C.: School of Public and International Affairs, George Washington University, pp. 65–85.

Pride, Richard A. and Gary L. Wamsley. 1972. Symbol Analysis of Network Coverage of the Laos Incursion. *Journalism Quarterly* 49 (Winter 1972): 635–640.

Raab, Earl. 1974. Is Israel Losing Popular Support? *Commentary* 57 (January 1974): 26–29.

Randal, Jonathan C. 1979. Captors Are Adept Media Manipulators. *Washington Post*, December 11, 1979.

Robinson, Michael J. and Karen A. McPherson. 1977. Television News Coverage Before the 1976 New Hampshire Primary. *Journal of Broadcasting* 21 (Spring 1977): 177–186.

Rubin, Barry. 1977. *International News and the American Media*. Beverly Hills, Ca.: Sage.

———· 1975. The Media and the Middle East. *Middle East Review* 7 (Winter 1975–76): 28–32.

Russo, Frank D. 1971. A Study of Bias in TV Coverage of the Vietnam War. *Public Opinion Quarterly* 35 (Winter 1971–72): 539–543.

Said, Edward W. 1980. Iran. *Columbia Journalism Review* 18 (March/April 1980): 23–33.

Sawyer, Kathy. 1980. Bodies Display. *Washington Post*, April 29, 1980.

Scammon, Richard M. and Ben J. Wattenberg. 1970. *The Real Majority*. New York: Berkley.

Schardt, Arlie. 1979. TV Held Hostage? *Newsweek* 94 (December 24, 1979): 24.

Shales, Tom. 1979. Terrorvision. *Washington Post*, December 11, 1979.

————· 1981. Stunning and Sublime: TV's Day of Drama. *Washington Post*, January 21, 1981.

————· 1981. The Great Welcome, With Trumpets. *Washington Post*, January 28, 1981.

Sreebny, Daniel. 1979. American Correspondents in the Middle East: Perceptions and Problems. *Journalism Quarterly* 56 (Summer 1979): 386–388.

Sterling, Christopher H. and Timothy R. Haight. 1978. *The Mass Media: Aspen Institute Guide to Communication Industry Trends*. New York: Praeger.

Suleiman, Michael W. 1965. An Evaluation of Middle East News Coverage of Seven American News Magazines, July-December 1956. *Middle East Forum* 41 (Autumn 1965): 9–30.

————· 1970. American Mass Media and the June Conflict. In Ibrahim Abu-Lughod, ed., *The Arab-Israeli Confrontation of June 1967*. Evanston, Ill.: Northwestern University Press, 138–154.

Tehran's Reluctant Diplomats. 1979. *Time* 114 (December 3, 1979): 64–67.

Terry, Janice. 1971. A Content Analysis of American Newspapers, In Abdeen Jabara and Janice Terry, eds., *The Arab World from Nationalism to Revolution*. Wilmette, Ill.: Medina University Press International, pp. 94–113.

————· 1973. US Press Coverage of the Middle East. *Journal of Palestine Studies* 4 (Autumn 1974): 120–133.

Tyrell, R. Emmett, Jr. 1981. News or Soap Opera. *Washington Post*, January 26, 1981.

Van Riper, Frank. 1981. Freed Hostages give Top Ratings to 'Special' TV News. *Chicago Tribune*, February 3, 1981.

Wagner, Charles H. 1973. Elite American Newspaper Opinion and the Middle East: Commitment versus Isolation. In Willard A. Beling, ed., *The Middle East: Quest for American Policy*. Albany, N.Y.: SUNY Press, pp. 306–334.

Weinraub, Bernard. 1980. Attention in U.S. Said to Drop After Iran's Expulsion of Journalists. *New York Times*, January 26, 1980.

# 2

## MEDIA SUPPORT FOR ISRAEL:
## A SURVEY OF LEADING JOURNALISTS

### S. ROBERT LICHTER

Studies of news media "bias" share an underlying assumption that the values and attitudes of journalists and broadcasters somehow influence their transmission of the news. Yet more research has concentrated on the product rather than the producers of the news. Television news broadcasts are widely monitored, especially during national political campaigns (Patterson & McClure, 1976; Hofstetter, 1976), but also to ascertain television's treatment of such controversial issues as Vietnam (Bailey, 1976; Braestrup, 1977), nuclear power (Efron, 1976; Media Institute, 1979), and race relations (Pride & Clark, 1973; Roberts, 1975; Civil Rights Commission, 1977). Although some of these scholars simply analyze the televised images they examine, others explicitly link their findings to attitudes within the journalistic community. Efron, for example, claims that the networks' "anti-nuclear" perspective is the product of widespread opposition to nuclear power among broadcast journalists.

Empirical data on such questions is rather sparse, in part because journalists take their claims of objectivity and professionalism in reporting the news very seriously. That is, they claim either to have no subjective viewpoint at all on their subject matter or, at worst, to be able to divorce their personal biases from their professional activities. Of course, the matter is considerably more complex, for a great middle ground lies between Agnewsque conspiracy theories and ritualized claims of objectivity (Tuchman, 1972). Social scientists are well aware that "reality" is not simply a given, and that all people, including social scientists and journalists, tend to view reality selectively. The selective perception of reality is influenced by many factors, one of which may be social ideology. Thus Agnew's charge of "liberal" media bias could, in theory, be disproven by findings that key media personnel hold predominantly conservative political outlooks. On the other hand, a finding that media personnel are liberal would not in itself prove his case. In fact, surveys reveal that leading journalists do tend to view society from a relatively liberal or leftist perspective (Barton, 1972; Johnstone et al., 1976; Sussman, 1976). This datum alone, however, conveys no information about media coverage. A *prima facie* case for liberal "bias" would have to correlate liberal media attitudes on specific issues with coverage of those same issues. The more specific the linkage, the stronger the argument becomes.

Like the other major controversies of our time, the Middle East conflict has stimulated both popular and scholarly interest in the nature of press coverage. Most studies have concluded that the national media have treated the Israelis more favorably than the Arabs (AIPC, 1967; Howard, 1967; Farmer, 1968; Suleiman, 1965, 1970; Wagner, 1973; Zaremba, 1977). Some recent studies have suggested a shift toward more positive portrayals of the Arab side (Belkaoui, 1978; Gordon, 1975).

Despite the substantial literature on this topic, however, there exists little basis for even a rudimentary linkage of journalists' attitudes with their output. The surveys cited above did not deal with this issue. We do know that Americans of Jewish background tend to be disproportionately represented in major mass media outlets (Rothman & Lichter, 1981). Although Jews constitute less than three percent of the American population, they make up a quarter of the Washington press corps (Sussman, 1976). In his classic organizational study of television news, Epstein mentions that 58 percent of the network producers and editors he interviewed were of Jewish descent (1973, p. 222–23). It is not known, however, whether these individuals are particularly pro-Israeli in their attitudes, much less in their presentations of the Middle East news over the air.

Despite the longstanding interest of scholars in media coverage of the Middle East conflict, there has existed no evidence to link this coverage to attitudes by media personnel. This article will present one such piece of evidence, drawn from a recent study of leading journalists and broadcasters at national news media outlets. As part of a much broader survey, these subjects were asked their opinions concerning America's obligation to defend Israel against its adversaries. Before examining their responses, the methods and research procedures used in this study will be described, so that readers can gauge for themselves the context and significance of the results.

## METHODOLOGY

The target group of this research consisted of those individuals who constitute the "national news media elite." The media elite population was defined as individuals having substantive input into news and public affairs content at the media outlets most influential in forming opinion within other national elites. The following organizations were sampled: *The New York Times, The Wall Street Journal, Time, Newsweek, U.S. News and World Report,* the news departments at ABC, CBS, and NBC, and the news and public affairs departments of PBS and three major public broadcasting stations, WNET in New York, WGBH in Boston, and WETA in Washington, D.C. (For evidence that these outlets are the most influential on national issues see AIPC, 1972; Johnstone, Slawski and Bowman, 1976; Lapham, 1973; Rivers, 1965, 1970; Sigal, 1973; Weiss, 1974). Relevant personnel in the print medium were reporters, columnists, department heads, bureau chiefs, editors, and executives with responsibility for news content. Those sampled from news broadcasting were correspondents and anchorpersons, producers, film editors, and news executives.[1]

We used a stratified probability sampling strategy, randomizing within organizations. Most of these subjects consider themselves independent professionals, rather than members of a corporate hierarchy. Therefore we contacted each of them individually rather than approaching top management for permission to survey its employees. All subjects in the sample first received a letter from the principle investigators asking them to participate in a study of social leadership. The letter was followed by a telephone call from an interviewer, who arranged an appointment. Most of those contacted agreed to be interviewed and successfully completed the questionnaire. On the average, the sessions lasted about 90 minutes. The interviews were conducted during the fall and winter of 1979–80.[2]

For a comparison group, 216 business executives were interviewed. We first secured the permission of parent companies to survey their employees. Otherwise, the sampling and interview procedures followed the format used for the media sample, and the interviews were conducted during the same time period. To represent the business elite, we sampled the top and

[1] This survey was conducted by Response Analysis, a survey research organization, under the direction of the present author and Stanley Rothman of Smith College, the senior investigator. The study was conducted under the auspices of the Research Institute of International Change at Columbia University. Funding was provided by the Alcoa Foundation, Earhart Foundation, Harry Frank Guggenheim Foundation, Sarah Scaife Foundation, and the Institute for Educational Analysis.

[2] Of the 340 journalists in the sample, 82 would not consent to be interviewed, a refusal rate of 24 percent. Another 20 could not be contacted during the time allotted for the survey. If we include these subjects as non-respondents, the completion rate drops from 76 percent to 71 percent of the entire sample. This is a very satisfactory response rate, especially since the interviews required substantial amounts of time and effort from a leadership group not always known for its cooperation with social scientific researchers. By comparison, the Harvard-*Washington Post* survey, which used a much briefer mail questionnaire, reported response rates ranging from 50 percent to 65 percent among the eight elites they surveyed (Sussman, 1976). The investigators did not specify the specific return rate for the media sample. Similarly, Kadushin's study of the American "intellectual elite" was based on a response rate of 54 percent, which the authors term "usual for such respondents" (Kadushin, 1974).

middle management of seven *Fortune 500* corporations drawn from all major sectors of the economy. The firms included a multinational oil company, a major bank, a public utility with plants in several states, a "fast-growth" company in the computer industry, a nationwide retail chain, a "high-technology" firm in the aerospace industry, and a highly diversified multinational corporation. Among this group a response rate of 96 percent was obtained. While this paper focuses primarily on the media elite, the business sample provides a valuable comparison group.

## MEDIA ELITE OPINION ON ISRAEL'S DEFENSE

All respondents completed a questionnaire that contained items and tests dealing with their personal backgrounds, motivations, perceptions, and attitudes toward current social and political issues. Of special interest are their responses to the following key statement with which they were asked to indicate strong agreement, mild agreement, mild disagreement, or strong disagreement:

The United States has a moral obligation to prevent the destruction of Israel.

This phrasing was intended to capture a commitment that goes beyond generalized expressions of support and encompasses a willingness to defend Israel in situations that might involve military strife. The statement also asserts that such a commitment is moral rather than merely pragmatic. On both counts, this is a relatively strong statement of support for Israel. It was intended to differentiate loyal and committed supporters from those who only sympathize with Israel.

Notwithstanding this "strong" phrasing, we found a widespread commitment to Israel among the media elite. Of the 238 respondents, 235 were willing to express an opinion. Fully 72 percent agreed that the United States was morally obligated to defend Israel, with over one in three (34 percent) indicating strong agreement with that proposition. Of the remaining 28 percent who disagreed, only 8 percent strongly disagreed. Thus, the vast majority of these leading journalists could be counted as staunch defenders of Israel. Conversely, a relative handful strongly rejected America's commitment to Israel's defense. Given the importance of these respondents as gatekeepers of public information, this is a striking finding.

This level of support was quite stable, cutting across occupational functions in both visual and print media. Dividing the sample into print and broadcast personnel produced almost exactly the same patterns of opinion in the two media. In no response category did the two groups differ by more than two percent, and the levels of strong support and opposition to Israel's defense differed by less than one percent. Nor was opinion distributed according to job functions. Dividing the sample into editors, reporters, television producers, on-camera personnel (correspondents and anchors), and network news executives also failed to produce statistically significant cleavages of opinion.

Despite this generalized support for Israel, one would expect opinion on this issue to divide along religious lines. Table 2.1 shows that Jews were by far the strongest supporters of Israel. Of those subjects who expressed a religious preference, over 90 percent of the Jews asserted a moral obligation to defend Israel, compared to 75 percent among Catholics and 71 percent among Protestants.[3] Moreover, the greatest differences occurred among those who strongly agreed with this position. Over half the Jews (54 percent) fell into this category, compared to about one-third of the Protestants (37 percent) and Catholics (32 percent). Even these results understate the impact of Jewish journalists on opinion within the media elite, however, because more than half the sample (52 percent) had no current religious affiliation.[4] Thus only thirty-three subjects, or 14 percent of those registering an opinion, were classified as Jewish.

To assess more accurately the effect of a Jewish *background* on attitudes toward Israel, subjects were reclassified into two groups: those who identified their parents as Jewish, and those whose ethnic origins were non-Jewish. As Table 2.2 shows, this procedure doubled the proportion of subjects classified as Jewish, from 14 to 28 percent. Thus the proportion of individuals of Jewish background in the media elite sample is about nine times that of the general population. Moreover, this group was almost as pro-Israeli as the smaller group of religiously affiliated Jews. Fully 85 percent supported Israel, and just under half (48 percent) qualified as strong supporters.

Among non-Jewish journalists the support level remained high. Two-thirds agreed with the commitment. Nonetheless, support among the Jewish group significantly exceeded that among the non-Jews. It seems fair to conclude that the media elite is strongly pro-Israeli, and that the degree of support is intensified by the large Jewish contingent within this leadership group.

## THE PUBLIC AND THE MEDIA ELITE

It might be argued that the media elite's commitment to Israel's defense is hardly surprising, given the American public's longstanding sympathy toward Israel. Thus the media leadership's pro-Israeli stance

---

[3] The statistical insignificance of these group differences stems from the lack of variation in opinion among Protestant, Catholic, and non-religious subjects. When these categories were collapsed into a single non-Jewish classification, the resultant differences were significant at .01 (cf. Table 2.2).

[4] By way of contrast, only 12 percent of the respondents in the business elite had no current religious affiliation.

**Table 2.1**
**Media Elite Attitudes Toward US Defense**
**of Israel by Current Religious Affiliation**

|  | Jewish | Protestant | Catholic | None |
|---|---|---|---|---|
| Strong support* | 55% | 37% | 32% | 29% |
| Support | 36 | 35 | 43 | 39 |
| Oppose | 9 | 20 | 21 | 22 |
| Strong oppose | 0 | 8 | 4 | 11 |
|  | 100% | 100% | 100% | 100% |
| (N) | (33) | (49) | (28) | (119) |

* Strong support indicates strong agreement with the statement, "The US has a moral obligation to prevent the destruction of Israel;" strong opposition indicates strong disagreement with this statement, etc.

$p = n.s$

**Table 2.2**
**Media Elite Attitudes Toward US Defense**
**of Israel by Ethnic Background**

|  | Jewish | Non-Jewish |
|---|---|---|
| Strong support | 48% | 29% |
| Support | 37 | 38 |
| Oppose | 12 | 23 |
| Strong oppose | 3 | 10 |
|  | 100% | 100% |
| (N) | (65) | (170) |

$p < .02$

might simply be viewed as a reflection of opinion among the populace. Polling data, however, suggest that the media elite's commitment to Israel exceeds the support shown by the general public. Since the Six Day War in 1967, Gallup and other national polling organizations have regularly asked Americans whether their sympathies lay more with the Israelis or the Arabs. During that time, pro-Israeli sentiment has outstripped pro-Arab feelings by ratios ranging from five to one to a commanding ten to one, although a large share of the public say "neither side." Sympathy toward Israel has never exceeded the 56 percent level measured just after the Six Day War, and it has dropped sharply since Sadat's 1977 visit to Israel, dipping as low as 33 percent in a 1978 Gallup poll conducted for *Newsweek* (Kohut, 1978).

At a time when sympathy for Israel had ebbed somewhat among the American public, the media elite's support level was quite high. Indeed the extent of their perceived obligation to defend Israel far exceeded the highest levels of sympathy ever recorded among the entire populace. Of course it is notoriously difficult to draw inferences about responses to differently phrased questions asked at different times among different groups. It is fairly safe to assume that the public's sense of obligation to defend Israel would not far exceed the proportion of Israeli sympathizers, but it is by no means certain.

Unfortunately, no national poll has ever used the precise phrasing we chose for our survey. On several occasions, however, the Harris organization measured sentiment for sending US troops to prevent Israel from being "taken over" or "overrun." Public support for US troop involvement never exceeded the level of 34 percent recorded after the 1973 war (Lipset & Schneider, 1977).

A fairer comparison with our own survey is offered by an NBC News survey, which provided a greater number of options for fulfilling any commitment to Israel. A national sample was asked in November 1977 whether the US should respond to an Arab attack on Israel by sending troops, giving unlimited military aid short of troops, giving limited military aid, giving no help to either party, or giving military assistance to the Arabs. In the wake of Sadat's peace initiative, only 4 percent were willing to commit troops to Israel's defense. Another 24 percent opted for unlimited aid aside from troops, and 17 percent would send limited supplies. The largest number, 39 percent, chose to stay out altogether, and 1 percent favored aiding the Arabs. The remaining 15 percent were undecided. Overall, then, the proportion of the public willing to come to Israel's defense only slightly exceeded the proportion rejecting any aid, by 45 to 40 percent.

This margin of support is far lower than we found among the media elite. Again, such comparisons should be approached with caution. It is possible, for example, that the measure of media support for Israel would have been lower if the statement had spelled out military options involved in fulfilling an abstract obligation. So we cannot say with certainty that the media elite feels a greater obligation toward Israel than does the general public. Nonetheless, the evidence on this point is quite suggestive, if not conclusive. These comparisons with polling data failed to yield any evidence that the American public supports Israel as strongly as does the media elite, whether public support is measured as mere "sympathy" or as willingness to commit American support to Israel's defense.

## BUSINESS AND MEDIA ELITES

If the media elite's attitudes do not simply reflect sentiment within the general public, what else can account for their strongly pro-Israeli stance? To some degree, the answer lies in their social status. After reviewing a decade of polling results on public attitudes toward Israel, Lipset and Schneider (1977, p. 26) conclude that:

> in virtually all surveys, support for Israel has tended to increase with higher levels of education, income, and occupational status. . . . These

findings, consistently showing greater support for Israel among the better educated, the more affluent, and those in executive and professional positions, suggest that Israel has strong backing among the elite sectors...

The journalists and broadcasters we interviewed were highly educated, well paid professionals. Their sense of obligation toward Israel is more in line with support levels among their socioeconomic peers than among the public at large. For example, a 1977 Roper poll showed that 54 percent of those in executive and professional occupations professed sympathy toward Israel, compared to 50 percent of white collar and 46 percent of blue collar workers. Similarly, in a winter 1974–75 Harris Survey, 54 percent of the college educated agreed that America has a special stake in seeing that Israel is not overtaken militarily, compared to 38 percent of the high school graduates and 30 percent of the grade school educated (Lipset & Schneider, 1977).

Even these results do not entirely account for the difference between the media elite and other groups. The journalists we surveyed seemed even more committed to Israel than the upper-status groups in these national polls. Fortunately, we need not rely entirely upon polling data to estimate these differences; our survey of business leaders allows precisely this kind of inter-elite comparison. Elite status can be controlled by comparing business and media leaders' perceived moral obligation to Israel's defense.

The result of this comparison is shown in Table 2.3, which crosstabulates attitudes toward Israel by membership in the two elite samples. As Lipset and Schneider's analysis would suggest, the business elite is also strongly supportive of Israel. By a margin of 60 to 40 percent, these corporate leaders feel morally obliged to come to Israel's defense. Nonetheless, the media elite remain significantly more pro-Israeli than even the business leaders. Differences between the two groups are found primarily at opposite ends of the opinion spectrum. Over one in three media leaders agree "strongly" that we should defend Israel, compared to less than one in four business leaders. Moreover, business executives are almost twice as likely as media personnel to strongly disavow any such commitment.

To what extent can these differences be attributed to the concentration of ethnic Jews in the media elite? Table 2.4 contrasts the two elites while holding Jewish ethnicity constant.

Among non-Jews, sympathy for Israel is somewhat stronger among the media leaders. They are almost half again as likely as the business leaders to feel strongly committed to Israel, by a margin of 29 to 20 percent. With Jewish subjects excluded from the comparison, however, the difference between media and business leaders fails to attain statistical significance. Moreover, Jews in the business elite are actually somewhat more pro-Israeli than are their journalistic counterparts.

Table 2.3
Elite Attitudes Toward US Defense
of Israel by Occupation

|  | Media | Business |
|---|---|---|
| Strong support | 35% | 23% |
| Support | 37 | 38 |
| Oppose | 20 | 24 |
| Strong oppose | 8 | 15 |
|  | 100% | 100% |
| (N) | (235) | (214) |

p<.03

Table 2.4
Elite Attitudes Toward US Defense of
Israel by Occupation, Controlling for Ethnicity

|  | Jews | | Non-Jews | |
|---|---|---|---|---|
|  | Media | Business | Media | Business |
| Strong support | 48% | 75% | 29% | 20% |
| Support | 37 | 17 | 38 | 39 |
| Oppose | 12 | 0 | 23 | 26 |
| Strong oppose | 3 | 8 | 10 | 15 |
|  | 100% | 100% | 100% | 100% |
| (N) | (65) | (12) | (170) | (202) |

p<.001

These results may seem paradoxical. How can it be that, with ethnicity controlled, the gap between the two elites narrows among the non-Jews and is actually reversed among those with Jewish backgrounds? The answer lies in the heavy representation of ethnic Jews in the media sample. The business elite contained only twelve Jews, less than six percent of those sampled, while the comparable figure for the media elite was 28 percent. Thus the media sample is composed of almost five times as many people of Jewish background as the business sample. In both professions, they are much stronger supporters of Israel than are non-Jews. The much higher proportion of Jews in the media sample increased the overall difference of opinion between the groups to the point where they became statistically significant. Were it not for the uneven distribution of people with Jewish backgrounds between the two elites, one could not have inferred from our sample data that the media elite is more pro-Israeli than the business elite.

Thus the media elite's commitment to Israel outstrips even that of other upper status groups, both because of the large proportion of Jews in the national media and because leading non-Jewish journalists are also relatively pro-Israeli. Of course, these two factors might be related; non-

Jewish journalists' attitudes toward Israel may well be influenced by the presence of such a substantial proportion of Jewish colleagues, most of whom are committed to Israel's defense.

## CONCLUSION

Our survey of leading journalists found widespread support for the proposition that America has a moral obligation to prevent Israel's destruction. Pro-Israeli sentiment within the media elite appears to extend well beyond the levels of support for Israel found among the general public, although precise comparisons are impossible. The strength of this sentiment can be explained in part by both the high social status of these individuals and the large proportion of ethnic Jews among them. Even when the effects of ethnic composition and social status are held constant, however, the media elite is characterized by strong support for Israel.

What should be inferred from these results? First, they should be treated with caution, because they are based on a single questionnaire item. This statement may have different meanings for different individuals, and there was no detailed question regarding specific foreign policy options.

Second, these findings do not prove that news stories in the national news media are "biased" toward the Israeli cause or against the Arabs. That issue can only be addressed by content analyses of media content, not by opinion surveys. Indeed a longstanding article of faith among journalists is that their professionalism precludes the intrusion of their own beliefs into their reportage. In some cases this view seems well founded. For example, although national media personnel tend to be political liberals and Democrats, most recent studies have failed to show any marked anti-Republican tilt in the coverage of political campaigns.

The question of values and news reporting requires research on a variety of issues and foci of reporting. Studies such as this one are a necessary prerequisite to determining whether any observed slant in Middle East coverage might be linked to a conscious or unconscious preference for one side. These findings do establish limitations on the viability of certain ideological explanations of coverage. For example, if Middle East coverage were found to be pro-Arab, such a conclusion could hardly be attributed to the sympathies of US journalists. However, a finding of pro-Israeli coverage, in conjunction with the attitudes found here, would not necessarily prove a direct linkage or "bias." It would first be necessary to eliminate a host of competing explanations that could account for the same phenomenon in terms of structural, situational, or other non-ideological influences (Epstein, 1973; Sigal, 1973; Weaver, 1976).

Michael Robinson has argued that a journalist with strong feelings about a controversial issue may be all the more likely to divorce personal opinions from reporting, because this is an acid test of the reporter's profes-sionalism. Robinson (1978, p. 204) writes, in reference to the topic at hand:

> . . . one might consider the relationship between news coverage of the Middle East and the religion or heritage of the correspondents. In this instance, the potential connection between background and story is so apparent that journalists would almost certainly be quite sensitive to potential bias. In a Middle East analysis, Jewish correspondents, recognizing the circumstance, would probably work hard to counter-act any attitudinal influences on their stories.

In charting the relationship between journalists' attitudes and out-puts, this factor must be remembered. Ultimately, the relation between a reporter's opinions and stories will be mediated by such personal qualities as sensitivity, introspection, and the ability to deal with the conscious and unconscious biases that are part of the human condition.

## REFERENCES

American Institute for Political Communication. 1967. *Domestic Communications Aspects of the Middle East Crisis*. Washington, D.C.: AIPC.

———· 1972. *The Credibility Problem: The Nixon Administration-Media Relationships*. Washington, D.C.: AIPC.

Bailey, George. 1976. Television War: Trends in Network Coverage of Vietnam 1965–70. *Journal of Broadcasting* 20 (Spring 1976): 147–58.

Barton, Alan. 1972. The American Leadership Study: Issues and Methods. Unpublished paper, mimeographed. New York: Columbia University.

Belkaoui, Janice Monti. 1978. Images of Arabs and Israelis in the Prestige Press, 1966–74. *Journalism Quarterly* 55 (Winter 1978): 732–38, 799.

Braestrup, Peter. 1977. *Big Story: How the American Press and Television Reported and Interpreted the Crisis of Tet 1968 in Vietnam and Washington*. Boulder, Colo.: Westview Press.

Civil Rights Commission. 1977. *Window Dressing on the Set: Women and Minorities in Television*. Washington, D.C.: U.S. Government Printing Office.

Efron, Edith. 1976. Nuclear Catastrophe? *Barron's* (June 7, 1976): 3, 18–26.

Farmer, Leslie. 1968. All We Know is What We Read in the Papers. *Middle East Newsletter* (February 1968): 1–5.

Hofstetter, Richard. 1976. *Bias in the News: Network Television Coverage of the 1972 Election Campaign*. Columbus: Ohio State University Press.

Howard, Harry N. 1967. The Instant Potboilers and the "Blitzkreig" War. *Issues* 21 (Autumn 1967): 48–52.

Johnstone, J.W., Edward J. Slawski and William W. Bowman. 1976. *The News People*. Bloomington: University of Illinois Press.

Kadushin, Charles. 1974. *The American Intellectual Elite*. Boston: Little, Brown.

Kohut, Andrew. 1978. American Opinion on Shifting Sands. *Public Opinion* 2 (May–June 1978): 15–18.

Lipset, S.M., and William Schneider. 1977. Carter vs. Israel: What the Polls Reveal. *Commentary* 64 (November 1977): 21–29.

Media Institute. 1979. *Television Evening News Covers Nuclear Energy: A Ten Year Perspective*. Washington, D.C.: The Media Institute.

Patterson, Thomas and Robert McClure. 1976. *The Unseeing Eye: The Myth of Television Power in National Politics*. New York: G.P. Putnam's Sons.

Pride, Richard, and Daniel Clark. 1973. Race Relations in Television News: A Content Analysis of the Networks. *Journalism Quarterly* 50 (Summer 1973): 319–28.

Rivers, William. 1965. *The Opinionmakers*. Boston: Little, Brown.

———· 1970. *Adversaries: Politics and the Press*. Boston: Beacon Press.

Roberts, Churchill. 1975. The Presentation of Blacks in Television Network Newscasts. *Journalism Quarterly* 52 (Spring 1975): 50–55.

Robinson, Michael. 1978. Future Television News Research: Beyond Edward J. Epstein. In William Adams and Fay Schreibman, eds., *Television Network News: Issues in Content Research*. Washington, D.C.: School of Public and International Affairs, George Washington University: 197–212.

Rothman, Stanley, and Robert Lichter. 1981. *Radical Christians, Radical Jews*. New York: Oxford University Press.

Sigal, Leon V. 1973. *Reporters and Officials: The Organization and Politics of Newsmaking*. Lexington, Mass.: D.C. Heath.

Suleiman, Michael W. 1965. An Evaluation of Middle East News Coverage in Seven American News Magazines, July–December 1956. *Middle East Forum* 41 (Autumn 1965): 9–30.

————. 1970. American Mass Media and the June Conflict. In Ibrahim Abu-Lughod, ed. *The Arab Israeli Confrontation of June 1967: An Arab Perspective*. Evanston, Ill.: Northwestern University Press: 138–54.

Sussman, Barry. 1976. *Elites in America*. Washington, D.C.: The Washington Post.

Tuchman, Gaye. 1972. Objectivity as Strategic Ritual: An Examination of Newsmen's Notion of Objectivity. *American Journal of Sociology* 77 (January 1972): 660–79.

Wagner, Charles H. 1973. Elite American Newspaper Opinion and the Middle East: Commitment versus Isolation. In Willard A. Beling, ed. *The Middle East: Quest for an American Policy*. Albany, N.Y.: SUNY Press: 306–44.

Weaver, Paul. 1972. Is Television News Biased? *The Public Interest* 26 (Winter 1972): 57–74.

Weiss, Carol. 1974. What America's Leaders Read. *Public Opinion Quarterly* 38 (Spring 1974): 1–22.

Zaremba, Alan Jay. 1977. An Exploratory Analysis of National Perceptions of the Arab-Israeli Conflict as Represented Through World Newspapers: An International Communications Study. PhD. Dissertation at State University of New York, Buffalo, 1977.

# 3

## SADAT GOES TO JERUSALEM:
## TELEVISED IMAGES, THEMES, AND AGENDA

### MAGDA BAGNIED
### STEVEN SCHNEIDER

On November 19, 1977, Egyptian President Anwar el-Sadat stepped off his plane in Jerusalem. Sadat's historic arrival was viewed by Israeli Prime Minister Menachem Begin, an Israeli honor guard, a cheering crowd, and millions of people around the world watching the event on television. Nearly every step of the journey was televised.

This study examines US network television news coverage of Sadat's visit to Jerusalem and the events surrounding the trip. First, we review trends in reporting the Arab-Israeli conflict. We next analyze the significance the networks attached to the trip by virtue of its domination of the news agenda between November 9, 1977—the date when Sadat spoke to the Egyptian Parliament and declared his interest in peace talks with Israel —and December 1, 1977—the date of the first Arab conference held in opposition to Sadat's trip. Finally, we evaluate the images that were presented of Anwar Sadat and Menachem Begin and the major themes in news coverage of the event.

### ARAB-ISRAELI MEDIA COVERAGE

The Middle East has long been an object of interest to the American news media. Even in the late Sixties, the Middle East received more coverage than any other foreign affairs story with the exception of the war in Vietnam (Warner, 1968; Almaney, 1970). Since the establishment of the state of Israel, US media have been accused of a pro-Israel bias.

Batroukha (1961) concluded that the *New York Times* had favored Israel in its reporting of the early stages of the 1956 Middle East war. Similarly, during the last six months of 1956, seven major US news magazines were found to be pro-Israeli and anti-Arab (Suleiman, 1965). Suleiman maintained that there was a "reluctance on the part of the American press to criticize the Israelis" (1956, p. 11).

When Suleiman replicated his 1956 study in an analysis of news stories about the 1967 Middle East war, he assessed 84 percent of the reporting as either pro-Israeli or anti-Arab or both (1970, pp. 140–41). Israel was presented as working miracles in a kind of "David-Goliath" match. For example, reports often contrasted the large combined Arab populations with the small Israeli population rather than Israel's 300,000 troops to the 285,000 Arab troops. Other studies also concluded that the American media were pro-Israeli in covering the Six Day War (APIC, 1967; Belkaoui, 1978; Howard, 1967; Farmer, 1968).

Belkaoui (1978) found that in 1967 the Israelis were given a neutral image while Arabs were cast in a negative light. Israelis "were more likely to tell, say, or announce than to threaten or warn," while Arabs "tended to deliver messages in an aggressive, angry, or threatening style" (p. 736).

Another pro-Israeli verdict came from Wagner's (1973) review of editorials in major American dailies from the end of the 1967 war through 1969. Wagner found the *New York Times*, *Los Angeles Times*, and *Washington Post* editorials to show a "generally pro-Israeli tone" as well as a "preoccupation with achievement of a negotiated settlement" in the conflict (Wagner, 1973, p. 317; see also Terry, 1971, 1974).

Coverage of the 1973 war is often cited as a turning point in the slant of Middle East reporting and as a marked departure from approaches of the 1950s and 1960s. Although Zaremba (1977) did contend that the *New York Times* continued to treat the Arabs as aggressors, other studies found a strong trend toward more neutral coverage. Gordon (1975) conducted the first published study of network television news coverage of the Middle East and found the reports balanced.

According to Gordon, television news reporting of the 1973 war was neither consistently pro-Israeli nor pro-Arab. Gordon found some differences in the way the three networks treated the war, but he did not find any patterns that indicated an overall bias in coverage. Gordon's conclusions, however, must be considered in light of his methodology. For information on the content of news stories, Gorden relied entirely on the abstracts provided in Vanderbilt's *Television News Index and Abstracts*. He did not view videotapes from Vanderbilt and he did not hear audio tapes of the newscasts. While the *Index and Abstracts* are a thorough finding aid and a good source for data on the agenda and topic of news stories, Vanderbilt advises against use of the abstracts for precise evaluations of the content of news stories and prints a warning against such use in each month's edition of the *Index and Abstracts*.

Despite this important caveat, Gordon's study is consistent with others in suggesting a change in coverage at the time of the 1973 war.[1] Belkaoui (1978) argues that a significant shift in the tenor of Middle East reporting occurred following that war. The American "prestige press" no longer uniformly depicted Israelis as "heros" and Arabs as "villains." In fact, "Israelis were increasingly described as angry, upset, worried, and gloomy" (p. 737), while there were "discernable shifts" in the images of Arabs. In particular, "Anwar Sadat, while not completely without a negative side. . . is portrayed in a much more sympathetic manner in 1973 than was Nasser in 1967" (p. 737).

These studies strongly suggest that the American news media became decidedly less pro-Israel between the 1956 war and the 1973 war. In the years following the 1973 "turning point," new complaints were voiced: Some now said coverage was slanted against Israel (see, for example, "Are the Media Fair to Israel?", 1975; Kenen, 1976, 1977; Laquer, 1977).

Peter Jennings, then ABC Middle East correspondent, agreed with the view of a change in Middle East reporting in a 1976 interview. Jennings said (Ghareeb, 1976, pp. 127–28):

> Traditionally, I think, more coverage has been given to the Israeli side than to that of the Arabs. But, I think that this situation began to change—not dramatically, perhaps, but substantially—after the October War in 1973 and particularly after the Arab oil embargo against the United States. The news media generally have now taken a much more prolific if not always incisive look at the Arab world.

If Jennings and the academic studies are correct, then the stage was set for the media to display their new "neutral" or perhaps even "pro-Arab" look when, in November 1977, Egyptian President Sadat announced his intention to visit Jerusalem and meet with Israeli Prime Minister Begin. His dramatic journey, with a massive American media entourage, became a classic "media event" (O'Connor, 1977).

## METHODOLOGY

This study addresses three key questions:

1. To what extent did reports of the Sadat visit dominate the television news agenda before, during, and after the visit?

---

[1] Sreebny (1979) found that American correspondents strongly believed the quality of Middle East coverage had improved substantially since 1973 and that "the most obvious improvement is the number of foreign correspondents (Americans and non-Americans, full and part-time) working in the Middle East" (p. 388).

2.  What images were televised of the two key actors–Sadat and Begin?
3.  Were the themes in news reports more favorable to Israel or to Egypt?

To explore these issues, Vanderbilt's *Television News Index and Abstracts* were used to identify early evening network news stories on the subject of the Sadat trip. The period from Wednesday, November 9, 1977, through Thursday, December 1, 1977, was reviewed. News specials during this time frame were also noted, using the *Nielsen TV Index.*

The news stories were coded on a variety of variables, including network, time, placement, anchor, key reporters, key speakers, major and minor themes, sites and visual themes. For the heavy coverage of the five days immediately prior to the visit (November 11–15), the regular CBS and ABC early evening newscasts were given more intensive analysis.

It should be noted that the data used in this study were gathered independently by each author. This report represents a collaboration between the authors after the stage of data collection. Some parts are entirely the result of one author's work (cf., Schneider, 1980, and Bagnied, 1981), while other parts are a merger of overlapping research. One researcher worked at the Television News Study Center in the Gelman Library at George Washington University. The other author conducted her research at the University of Cairo, George Washington University, and the National Archives.

## DOMINATING THE NEWS

To have an impact on the national consciousness, news stories need to rank high on the news agenda. Stories that receive extensive coverage night after night are clearly most likely to be perceived as salient and significant. It seems probable that the images and themes of these saturation stories are likely to acquire important status in the public collective memory, regardless of the event's ultimate historical significance and its actual immediate and tangible consequences.

The story of Sadat's visit was given this sort of massive coverage; it clearly dominated network newscasts night after night for several weeks. A total of almost 25¼ hours of news stories and special reports were presented by ABC, CBS, and NBC during the 23 days that were analyzed.

Four phases of coverage were observed. During the first five days after Sadat's announced intention of making the trip (November 9–November 13), the story became the lead news item. In this period it was the lead on eight of the twelve newscasts and averaged about 1½ minutes in length (see Table 3.1).

Table 3.1
Network Evening Newscasts and Special Coverage of Sadat's Trip to Jerusalem

| Date | ABC | | | CBS | | | NBC | | |
|------|----------|---------|----------|----------|---------|----------|----------|---------|----------|
| | Position | Minutes | Per Cent | Position | Minutes | Per Cent | Position | Minutes | Per Cent |
| 11/9 | 1 | .2 | 1 | 1 | .3 | 1 | 1 | .5 | 2 |
| 11/10 | 5 | .3 | 1 | 1 | .3 | 1 | 7 | .2 | 1 |
| 11/11 | 3 | 1.2 | 6 | 2 | 2.0 | 9 | 1 | 3.0 | 14 |
| 11/12 | — | — | — | 1 | 3.4 | 15 | 1 | 2.3 | 10 |
| 11/13 | — | — | — | 1 | 2.4 | 10 | — | — | — |
| 11/14 | 1 | 3.6 | 16 | 1 | 8.2 | 35 | 1 | 5.0 | 26 |
| 11/15 | 2 | 6.9 | 32 | 2 | 4.7 | 20 | 1 | 6.9 | 28 |
| 11/16 | 1 | 5.7 | 23 | 1 | 5.9 | 26 | 1 | 6.8 | 30 |
| 11/17 | 1 | 8.8 | 40 | 1 | 13.9 | 60 | 1 | 8.2 | 37 |
| 11/18 | 1 | 14.4 | 65 | 1 | 11.5 | 51 | 1 | 11.7 | 52 |
| 11/19 | — | — | — | 1 | 17.3 | 75 | 1 | 12.7 | 55 |
| | (Live) | 75.0 | | (Live) | 60.0 | | (Live) | 95.0 | |
| | (Special) | 21.0 | | — | — | | — | — | |
| 11/20 | — | — | — | 1 | 6.4* | 59 | 1 | 40.1** | 91 |
| | (Live) | 210.0 | | (Live) | 180.0 | | (Live) | 181.0 | |
| | (Special) | 60.0 | | (Special) | 36.0 | | — | — | |
| 11/21 | 1 | 13.8 | 63 | 1 | 12.7 | 55 | 1 | 14.0 | 64 |
| | (Live) | 27.0 | | (Live) | 45.0 | | (Live) | 90.0 | |
| 11/22 | 1 | 10.5 | 48 | 1 | 15.6 | 66 | 1 | 5.6 | 25 |
| 11/23 | 3 | 7.5 | 34 | 1 | 6.8 | 30 | 1 | 5.8 | 26 |
| 11/24 | 10 | 3.7 | 16 | 1 | 4.6 | 20 | 7 | 2.0 | 16 |
| 11/25 | 3 | 2.6 | 12 | 2 | 4.1 | 18 | 5 | 7.6 | 35 |
| 11/26 | — | — | — | 1 | 9.4 | 41 | 1 | 16.2 | 70 |
| 11/27 | — | — | — | 1 | 8.7* | 77 | 1 | 6.5 | 30 |
| 11/28 | 1 | 4.5 | 21 | 1 | 9.7 | 42 | 1 | 6.8 | 31 |
| 11/29 | 11 | 3.3 | 15 | 3 | 3.5 | 15 | 3 | .7 | 3 |
| 11/30 | 1 | 5.9 | 27 | 1 | 8.0 | 35 | 1 | 6.1 | 28 |
| 12/1 | 1 | 4.9 | 22 | 1 | 5.5 | 24 | 4 | 3.8 | 17 |

* Late-evening, fifteen minute news program
** One-hour, early evening news program

The five days preceeding the trip saw a further buildup in coverage on all three networks. At this point, 36 percent of all regular newscast time was devoted to the Sadat trip, and it was the lead story on 13 of the 15 newscasts. Having prefaced the trip with such attention, the networks brought their coverage to a climax with a remarkable three days of satellite-dependent news on the actual days of the trip—November 19–21.

On the regular newscasts, Sadat's trip typically constituted almost two-thirds of the news time, and was invariably the lead story. In addition, the three networks broadcast nearly 17 hours of live coverage and nearly two hours of special reports during this intense three-day period.

Saturation coverage continued during the ten days following the trip. News about the visit and its repercussions led the newscasts on 18 of 28 times. Even in this period, over 30 percent of all available evening newscast time went to the Sadat story.

These four periods add up to an extraordinary amount of attention. Television news stories are usually relatively brief (less than three minutes) and are spread across a variety of subjects. When Lefever (1974) categorized CBS early evening, weekday newscasts for 1972 and 1973, only ten general topics garnered more than three hours of coverage during an entire year; these subjects included the '72 presidential campaign, the Vietnam war, Watergate, the economy, and all miscellaneous human interest stories. Yet, in about three weeks the Sadat story was given nearly three hours on regular CBS evening newscasts.

Research into the agenda-setting function of the mass media suggests that such coverage is highly significant. McCombs and Shaw (1977, p. 12) have explained that agenda setting refers to "a strong positive relationship between the emphases of mass communication and the salience of these topics to the individuals in the audience." Comstock (1978, p. 328) concludes his review of agenda-setting research with the observation that:

> Television...influences the degree of attention the public gives to topics, persons, and symbols, thereby affecting the conduct and outcome of political activity.

The "topics, persons, and symbols" that were highlighted by heavy coverage of these particular events are clear. The topic was the unprecedented meeting of the heads of government of Egypt and Israel, a meeting that was held in Jerusalem. To an event already filled with symbols, the networks added more symbols—from doves of peace in backdrops to dispatching their anchorpeople to accompany Sadat personally. As for the key persons, there were two—Sadat and Begin. For the first time, Americans had an extended opportunity to see an Arab leader in the role of peacemaker and as the recipient of considerable praise.

## VISUAL IMAGES OF SADAT AND BEGIN

Many observers were astonished at what they considered to be the powerful impact of the visual images in the news. John O'Conner in the *New York Times* (1977, p. 17) stressed the "unforgettable images" conveyed by television:

> The extraordinary event was largely symbolic, and therefore the function of television could clearly be seen in its most powerful aspects. President Anwar el-Sadat's historic trip to Israel apparently offered little in the way of concrete political resolutions, but it left the world with a new collection of unforgettable images.

Haynes Johnson in the *Washington Post* (1977, p. 3) similarly noted that this "was a case where images, pictures, and sound really were worth more than written words, where each of us could react personally to the sense of history happening before us. . ."

Of special interest was the media persona of each of the principles—Anwar Sadat and Menachem Begin. When recalling "indelible visual impressions," reporters and media critics alike turned to the images of Sadat and Begin. As Ted Koppel said on ABC (November 23, 1977):

> In the course of forty-eight hours, American television flooded the world with a series of indelible visual impressions: Sadat and Begin—men of courage, men of goodwill, men of peace. The substance of their discussions remains shrouded in mystery, but their television images alone created a new diplomatic reality and what was said is of far less importance at the moment than what was seen.

Systematic analysis of television's visual coverage has rarely been attempted. Adams (1978) has evaluated in some detail approaches to analysis of television visuals and has reviewed past efforts to study news visuals. He argues that newscast video images convey "information (factual and evaluative) beyond that asserted orally" and may sometimes send "competing and perhaps discrepant stimuli" (p. 169).

In the case of Sadat's trip to Israel, the images of Sadat and Begin assumed special importance. Some analysts were particularly impressed with Sadat's television presence. Meg Greenfield wrote (1977) that Sadat

> . . .has transformed more than the political landscape of the Middle East. He has surely also transformed, or at least substantially altered, the American perception of the Arab and his cause. Unlike the set pieces to which we have become accustomed—the oil rich sheik, the terrorist, the ululating crowd—Sadat was neither alarming nor strange. He was politically plausible and humanly familiar.

Diamond and Cassidy go further in evaluating Sadat's performance. Of the "unforgettable" media images, they wrote (1979, p. 7):

> The figures of Sadat and Begin represented a reversal of symbolic images. Urbane, pipe-smoking, English-speaking Sadat not only looked "Western" but sounded statesmanlike when he talked of peace. Begin, on the other hand, appeared as a remote even fanatical figure.

The American public apparently concurred with these perceptions of Sadat as both his recognition and popularity increased sharply after November, 1977. What can account for such reactions? Were there aspects of television's depictions of Sadat that promoted this favorable reception?

In order to investigate such questions, all of the on-camera airtime given Sadat and Begin on the regular evening newscasts from November 9 through December 1 were analyzed. A stopwatch was used to isolate and code only the seconds when one or both leaders were shown on camera.

Before examining the nature of the images that were presented, the basic finding regarding airtime is itself noteworthy.

Sadat was shown on camera more than twice as much as Begin during this period of saturation coverage. Over these 23 days all three networks' regular evening newscasts had just over 75 minutes of Anwar Sadat on camera compared to slightly less than 35 minutes of Menachem Begin. (It should be remembered that by television's standards of brief, fast-paced stories, in which "interviews" and film clips are measured in seconds not minutes and in which most time is taken by the correspondents and anchors, these totals represent substantial on-camera air time for both Sadat and Begin.)

This lopsided ratio of over 2:1 would not, however, entirely support the claim that it shows unfair treatment of Begin; in many respects, the event was understandably interpreted as Sadat's story. After all, in the "peace initiative," it was Sadat who made the trip. He was the first Arab leader to make such a gesture, and he was subjected to bitter threats from certain quarters. The findings would have been more surprising had Sadat not had some lead over Begin in total attention.

The pattern is more useful in another regard. Sadat's extensive exposure goes a long way toward explaining why the coverage seemed to influence his image so much more than it did that of Begin. Sadat was on the center stage of television much more frequently and longer than was Begin.

During the time when Sadat was on camera he was presented in ways that differed markedly from Begin. One dimension that was studied was on-camera "activity." How much was each leader shown speaking, interacting with the public, gesturing with arms and hands, sitting being interviewed, or shown as the recipient of public acclaim? These are not exhaustive and exclusive categories; rather, they are a series of dichotomous variables (e.g., time on-camera in interviews vs. time on-camera not devoted to interviews). Data were initially analyzed separately for each network, but the differences between networks were trivial, so the findings presented here are based on the totals for all three networks' evening newscasts.

In general, the findings suggest that Begin was disproportionately shown as more loquacious, aloof, and withdrawn than Sadat, who was shown as relatively more outgoing, open, gregarious, popular, and active. When Begin was pictured he was over twice as likely to have been shown lecturing groups of people as was Sadat. Begin was presented speaking to crowds, or groups of journalists, or addressing the Knesset for 43 percent of his on-camera airtime, while Sadat was shown "public speaking" only 20 percent of the time.

Sadat, far more than Begin, was depicted as being outgoing and interacting with people. Sadat was pictured mingling with informal groups of people, consulting with his aides, shaking hands, and listening carefully to the words of others in 21 percent of his on-camera time. Begin, who also customarily shakes hands with people, was shown in such activities only four percent of his on-camera time.

Reinforcing this pattern, Sadat was also observed receiving the acclaim of supportive crowds far more often than Begin. Sadat was pictured being applauded or cheered by welcoming crowds for a full 18 percent of the time he was on camera. Begin, on the other hand, was given such applause on only two percent of his airtime.

On yet another series of "activity" measures, Sadat's televised image surpassed Begin's. Sadat's air time showed him engaging over three times as much in such movements and gestures as waving, hugging and kissing, praying, and striding forward as did Begin's—seven percent versus two percent, respectively. Similarly, while six percent of Sadat's time on camera covered him riding triumphantly in motorcades, virtually no time was given to Begin in such a context. Sadat was even shown broadly smiling considerably more than Begin. Ten percent of the time Sadat was pictured with a clearcut smile, compared to six percent of the time for Begin.

These have all been relative comparisons using percentages. If the contrasts are made using absolute amounts of air time, differences in the portrayals are magnified further, because Sadat was the recipient of so much more overall time on camera. In absolute terms of news time, the image of Sadat as the more vigorous, admired, and affable of the two leaders is even greater because he received over twice as much on-camera coverage as Begin. For example, though Sadat was shown smiling nearly twice as much, proportionately, as was Begin, viewers actually saw a smiling Sadat four times as much as they saw a smiling Begin, because Sadat received over twice as much total airtime.

A number of other visual-image variables were coded and are analyzed in more detail elsewhere by Bagnied (1981). The findings from these variables lend additional evidence for a full appreciation of Sadat's and Begin's images. Sadat consistently emerged as the more visually open and expressive leader. While Begin tended to jab his hands up and down for emphasis, Sadat more often used a steady, open-palm gesture, sometimes opening wide his arms as well. On-camera, Begin waved his finger and pointed twice as often as did Sadat; the Egyptian leader frequently nodded his head in sympathy with the speaker and also cupped his ear to listen carefully (see Bagnied, 1981).

The point of these and the previous findings is of course not to try to assess the extent to which the edited televised versions of these men correctly reflected the way they "really were;" all television images are invariably a mixture of what Adams (1978) terms "production factors" and "event factors." Begin did suffer from the network reliance on the "talking head" setting for his airtime, while the more extensive coverage of Sadat captured him engaging in a variety of telegenic and positive activities.

The data analysis enabled us to identify some of the specific factors that contributed to Greenfield's sense of Sadat as "humanly familiar" and Diamond's impression that Begin was "remote." All of the findings pointed to a strong image of Sadat as an active, friendly, expressive, and popular leader, someone who listens and interacts as well as speaks. Begin, in contrast, was seen centrally as a non-interactive speaker, less frequently relating personally with other people, and almost never the beneficiary of positive crowd reactions. By way of gestures, actions, and context, Sadat's television persona suggested what, using Barber's typology of political leadership styles (1972), would be called "active-positive"—an enthusiastic and assertive leader initiating bold new policies.

Patterson and McClure (1976, p. 85) maintain that through "the use of dramatic pictures some events can forever be fixed in the viewer's mind." If so, from this episode the enduring pictures of Anwar Sadat are striking ones.

## THEMES PRIOR TO THE JOURNEY

The five days immediately preceeding Sadat's arrival in Jerusalem were especially important newscasts. As explained above, this period saw a major jump in coverage of news about the upcoming trip; almost every day it was the lead story on all networks. Stories about the imminent visit, reactions to its announcement, and speculation about its implications consumed more attention each passing day. By Friday, the day before the trip, over half the total newscasts on all three networks were devoted to Sadat's trip.

This buildup period established the themes of coverage, defined the issues, established the story lines, and reintroduced the principals to the American public. Inasmuch as television news tends to set up fairly simple and unambiguous "plots" (Epstein, 1973; Weaver, 1976) and tends to sustain initial themes and characterizations, this period is instructive to examine.

Two networks—CBS and ABC—were analyzed in detail. There were no important differences between the two, and the data reported here are based on the average of both networks. Major themes were coded and the amount of time devoted to each major theme was recorded.

The most repeated major theme during the week before Sadat's journey was that "non-Egyptian Arabs oppose the trip." Over one-third (34 percent) of all relevant news time echoed this theme. The shock and outrage of other Arab capitals were featured prominently. The most common epithet reported for Sadat was that of "traitor." CBS stories, for example, quoted the term as being used by leftist Palestinians marching in Beirut, Syrian and

Libyan governments, PLO leaders in Damascus, and other Arab "rejectionists."

The implications of this emphasis on Arab hostility to the trip are threefold: First, it dramatically highlighted an emergent distinction between Egypt and the undifferentiated "Arab world," and between Sadat and the unreconstructed Arab leaders. Second, it increased the perception of Sadat as "courageous" to go to Jerusalem in the face of such virulent opposition. And third, the emphasis on "rejectionist" Arab anger did not extend to giving any credence to their views; the American media accepted Sadat's trip as an unquestionably worthwhile step toward peace in the Middle East. Consequently, any opposition to the trip was treated as negative news.

The second most frequently voiced theme was that "Israelis support Sadat's trip," 11 percent of the news time fell into this category. Again, much of this coverage was replete with praise for Sadat. Israelis were said to "be touched by Sadat's magnificent gesture and by the courage he showed" (CBS).

The next two most common themes concerned the initiation of what the networks called a "daring venture," "courageous step," "momentous visit," "bold gamble," "stunning breakthrough," "dramatic gesture," and "historic occasion." Some stories treated the trip as entirely Sadat's initiative, while others gave Begin credit with Sadat. (In no instance was the trip attributed solely to Begin's initiative.) Ten percent of the news time emphasized the trip as the product of the joint efforts of both men. However, another nine percent stressed that Sadat alone launched the venture. Thus, Sadat was portrayed as sharing the olive branch with Begin only slightly more than he was given full credit for first offering the olive branch.

The theme that "Americans support Sadat's trip" was aired seven percent of the time, creating a Western consensus favoring the visit. There was no other single major theme that was dominant in more than five percent of the stories, and many of the remaining stories did not have a clearcut major theme.

## CONCLUSION

Did the coverage given Sadat's trip to Jerusalem represent a change in television's treatment of Arab-Israeli conflict? Does it lend support to the notion that the American media were not as pro-Israeli as previous studies, especially those prior to the 1973 war, had found them to be? Paradoxically, the answer is a qualified "no," despite the favorable coverage of Sadat.

The extension of favorable coverage to Sadat did not come at Israel's direct expense. Instead, television news lifted Sadat, the peace pilgrim, above the other Arabs who appeared to reject any negotiation with Israel.

Such coverage did not depart from the traditional treatment given most of the rest of the Arab world. In this sense, reporting of the trip remained consistent with twenty years of Middle East news. Change in the coverage of Sadat coincided with the change in his approach toward Israel and does not, in itself, offer evidence for any marked change in the tenor of Middle East coverage.

Ironically, however, Sadat's ascension in television news put into place a highly visible, articulate voice that was treated as a credible alternative to Begin. Sadat's image was solidified as a "Westernized," rational, peaceful, personable leader, sufficiently legitimate to appear on a warm, first-name basis with Cronkite and Walters. Having acquired that status, Sadat was then able to speak to Americans, in modulated and moderate tones, on such charged issues as the Palestinian problem. Although he was being attacked by some Arabs for his efforts, Sadat emerged in American television as the first Arab leader able to validate as worthy of discussion most of the key Arab complaints about the state of Israel.

## REFERENCES

Adams, William C. 1978. Visual Analysis of Newscasts: Issues in Social Science Research. In William Adams and Fay Schreibman, eds. *Television Network News: Issues in Content Research*. Washington, D.C.: School of Public and International Affairs, George Washington University, pp. 154–73.

Almaney, Adnan. 1970. International and Foreign Affairs on Network Television News. *Journal of Broadcasting* 14 (Fall 1970): 499–509.

American Institute for Political Communication. 1967. *Domestic Communications Aspects of the Middle East Crisis*. Washington, D.C.: APIC.

Are The Media Fair To Israel? 1975. *Near East Report* 19 (February 5, 1975): 22.

Bagnied, Magda. 1981. American Network Television Coverage of President Sadat's Peace Initiative. Ph.D. dissertation, Cairo University.

Barber, James David. 1972. *The Presidential Character*. Englewood Cliffs, N.J.: Prentice Hall.

Batroukha, Mohammed Ezzedin. 1961. The Editorial Attitudes of the *New York Times* and the *Christian Science Monitor* Toward the Arab-Israeli Dispute (January 1, 1955–June 30, 1956): A Content Analysis Study. Ph.D. dissertation, Syracuse University.

Belkaoui, Janice Monti. 1978. Images of Arabs and Israelis in the Prestige Press. 1966–1974. *Journalism Quarterly* 55 (Winter 1978): 732–38, 799.

Comstock, George, Steven Chaffee, Nathan Katzman, Maxwell McCombs, & Donald Roberts. 1978. *Television and Human Behavior*. New York: Columbia University Press.

Diamond, Edwin & Paula Cassidy. 1979. Arabs vs. Israelis, Has television taken sides? *TV Guide* (January 6, 1979): 7.

Farmer, Leslie. 1968. All We Know is What We Read in the Papers. *Middle East Newsletter* (February 1968): 1–5.

Ghareeb, Edmund. 1976. The American Media and the Palestinian Problem. *Journal of Palestine Studies* 5 (Fall–Winter 1976): 127–49.

Gordon, Avishag H. 1975. The Middle East October 1973 War as Reported by the American Networks. *International Problems* 14 (Fall 1975): 76–85.

Greenfield, Meg. 1977. Our Ugly Arab Complex. *The Washington Post* (November 30, 1977): A-23.

Howard, Harry N. 1967. The Instant Potboilers and the "Blitzkrieg" War. *Issues* 21 (Autumn 1967): 48–52.

Johnson, Haynes. 1977. Historic Meeting of Heads of State. *Washington Post* (November 22, 1977): 17.

Kenen, I. L. 1977. Monitor: Jerusalem Distorted. *Near East Report* 21 (June 15, 1977): 100.

———· Kenen, I. L. 1976. Monitor: Petrodollars and the Media. *Near East Report* 20 (June 2, 1976): 102.

Laquer, Walter. 1967. Israel, the Arabs, and World Opinion. *Commentary* 44 (August 1967): 49–59.

Lefever, Ernest. 1974. *TV and National Defense: An Analysis of CBS News, 1972–73.* Boston, Virginia: Institute for American Strategy.

O'Conner, John J. 1977. TV: Symbolic Event is Highlighted by "Sheer Drama of Pictures." *New York Times* (November 2, 1977): 17:3.

Patterson, Thomas E. & Robert D. McClure. 1976. *The Unseeing Eye: The Myth of Television Power in National Politics.* New York: G.P. Putnam's Sons.

Schneider, Steven M. 1980. A Content Analysis of Sadat's 1977 Visit to Israel. In Richard L. Cole. *Introduction to Political Inquiry.* New York: Macmillan Publishing Company, pp. 245–59.

Shaw, Donald L. & Maxwell McCombs. 1977. *The Emergence of American Political Issues.* St. Paul: West Publishing.

Sreebny, Daniel. 1979. American Correspondents in the Middle East: Problems and Perceptions. *Journalism Quarterly* 56 (Summer 1979): 386–88.

Suleiman, Michael W. 1965. An Evaluation of Middle East News Coverage of Seven American News Magazines, July–December 1956. *Middle East Forum* 41 (Autumn 1965): 9–30.

———· 1970. American Mass Media and the June Conflict. In Ibrahim Abu-Lughod, ed. *The Arab Israeli Confrontation of June 1967: An Arab Perspective.* Evanston, Ill.: Northwestern University Press, 138–54.

Terry, Janice. 1971. A Content Analysis of American Newspapers. In Abdeen Jabara and Janice Terry, eds. *The Arab World from Nationalism to Revolution.* Wilmette, Illinois: Medina University Press International.

———· 1974. 1973 US Press Coverage on the Middle East. *Journal of Palestine Studies* 4 (Autumn 1974): 120–33.

Wagner, Charles H. 1973. Elite American Newspaper Opinion and the Middle East: Commitment versus Isolation. In Willard A. Beling, ed. *The Middle East: Quest for an American Policy.* Albany, N.Y.: SUNY Press, pp. 306–34.

Warner, Malcolm. 1968. TV Coverage of International Affairs. *Television Quarterly* 7 (Spring 1968): 60–75.

Zaremba, Alan Jay. 1977. An Exploratory Analysis of National Perceptions of the Arab-Israeli Conflict as Represented Through World Newspapers: An International Communications Study. Ph.D. disseration, State University of New York, Buffalo.

# 4

## ARABS, ISRAELIS, AND TV NEWS: A TIME-SERIES, CONTENT ANALYSIS

### MORAD ASI

According to published studies, Arabs and Islam have been portrayed unfavorably by the American mass media and perceived negatively by the American public. Studying high school textbooks, Perry (1965) discovered that Islam was presented as an intolerant religion and that Arabs were shown as nomads. Nasir (1976) concluded that Arabs were viewed in the U.S. mass media as an "outgroup" whose religious and cultural values were alien to the West. Such findings led Suleiman (1977, p. 10) to conclude:

> The Western picture of the Arab has been built up, not through familiarity, but over a long period in which Arabs have appeared variously as non-Christian fanatics fighting Crusaders; as the protagonists of fictitious romantic episodes such as those of *Arabian Nights*...as the source of violent headlines in contemporary newspapers, and, most recently, as the cause of the sudden...embargo on oil to the U.S.

In recent years, television news has become the primary source on which most Americans claim to rely for international news, and consequently, is a key source for images of the Arab nations and conflicts in the Middle East. Because so much of the news from the Middle East has centered on the Arab-Israeli conflict, it is useful to contrast the portrayals of Arabs and Arab states with those of Israelis and the state of Israel.

Previous studies have suggested that during the 1970s media coverage of the Middle East (especially coverage in the printed media) became less pro-Israeli and more neutral. Bagnied and Schneider (1981) have reviewed some of the studies, but comparing different studies with different measures and sometimes different news outlets to draw time-series conclusions is of course a difficult enterprise. More longitudinal research is needed. As Patterson (1978, p. 183) maintained: "Many studies of television news could benefit by incorporating a time dimension into the research design."

Adams and Heyl (1981) show earlier in this volume that two key media events in the Arab-Israeli conflict during the 1970s were the 1973 war and Egyptian President Anwar Sadat's visit to Israel in November 1977. Because it has sometimes been argued that these two episodes were turning points in the US media's coverage of the Arab-Israeli saga, they mark very appropriate dates for the before-and-after analyses of television news treatments of Arabs and Israelis that were used in this study. The design that is outlined here is intended to test whether these events did operate as turning points in Middle East coverage and to examine the trends in coverage during the 1970s.

## METHODOLOGY

The research reported here was part of a larger study of network coverage of the Middle East during the 1970s (Asi, 1981).[1] The goal of this portion of the research was to determine how the leading Arab states and Israel were treated on ABC, CBS, and NBC, early evening, weekday newscasts during three different periods during the 1970s—in 1973 prior to the war, in 1976–77 after the war and before Sadat's trip, and in 1979 after Sadat's trip.

Note that the research did not directly examine coverage of the 1973 war or Sadat's 1977 visit, but rather focused on less extraordinary periods before and after these pivotal events. A total of fifteen weeks of Middle East coverage were content analyzed; five weeks were reviewed for each of the three periods. This amount of coverage was deemed sufficient for the purpose of assessing the direction (favorable-neutral-unfavorable) of coverage. For the weeks that were sampled, each weekday newscast for each network was analyzed.[2]

Five US-born graduate students at Ohio University performed the coding after having undergone two two-hour training sessions. The news story was used as the basic unit of analysis on the premise that the news story is "the smallest completely self-contained message in the news program" (Hofstetter, 1976, p. 27).

---

[1] For their help in the design and completion of the overall study, the author would like to thank Guido Stempel III, Graduate Coordinator for the School of Journalism, and Drew McDaniels, Director of the School of Radio and Television, both of Ohio University.

---

[2] The 1973 period consisted of April 23–27, May 28–June 1, July 4–8, August 6–10, August 13–17. The 1976–77 period covered November 22–26, 1976, and, in 1977, January 10–14, March 14–18, April 11–15, April 18–22. The 1979 period included January 22–26, February 19–23, April 23–27, August 27–31, September 24–28.

A five-point scale was developed with "very favorable" on one end and "very unfavorable" on the other. Almost 95 percent of the stories were placed in the middle three codes of favorable, neutral, or unfavorable, rather than extreme categories of "very favorable" or "very unfavorable." As a result, the presentation of data in the tables in this report merges the five categories into three: favorable, neutral, and unfavorable.

"Favorable" stories were those that reflected social cohesion and co-operation, political and economic stability and/or strength. In international affairs, stories about countries or their leaders were coded "favorable" if they were depicted as being just and/or cooperative. Coverage which described a country or its leaders as progressive, successful, peace-loving, moral, intelligent, lawful, unified, and/or exhibiting positive leadership was coded as favorable. (This classification was not assigned to any country, group, or leader characterized as exploiting strength over weaker nations, groups, or individuals.)

"Unfavorable" news stories were those that reported social conflict, disorganization, instability, and/or weakness. In international affairs, "unfavorable" stories were those indicating a country or its leaders were uncooperative, belligerent, wrong, and/or weak.

"Neutral" stories reflected neither a favorable nor unfavorable emphasis due to a balance of content or lack of controversial material. Overall intercoder reliability was 82 percent. For additional explanation of the methodology refer to Asi (1981; see also Budd, Donohew, and Thorp, 1967).

Videotapes for the research were secured from Vanderbilt University's Television News Archive after having located the relevant stories using Vanderbilt's *Television News Index and Abstracts*—a total of almost 183 stories on all three networks. The sample included 53 NBC stories, 63 CBS stories, and 69 ABC stories, although the network differences were not statistically significant.

The sample succeeded in obtaining a good mix of fairly "routine" Middle East news and not exclusively "crisis" coverage. Of the 183 stories, only 8 were lead stories and only 12 were in second position in the newscasts. Thus, about nine out of ten of the stories sampled were ranked third or later in the newscasts.

Just over 60 percent of these stories were from outside the studio, while about 40 percent were studio stories. In terms of visuals, 31.7 percent had only film; 35.0 percent had only graphics; 21.3 percent had both film and still graphics; and 12.0 percent had no visuals.

## COVERAGE CHANGES IN THE 1970s

Table 4.1 presents the number and percent of favorable, neutral, and unfavorable stories during the three periods under study for Israel, Egypt, the PLO, and all other Arab states. The latter category included stories about Saudi Arabia, Syria, and Lebanon, and references to "Arab countries" without mention of specific states. The table combines the ABC, CBS, and NBC totals, because there were no significant differences in the individual network tabulations.

A number of noteworthy patterns may be observed in these data:

1. Both Egypt and the PLO were the recipient of more favorable coverage in 1979 than earlier in the 1970s;
2. Coverage of Israel, however, was less favorable in 1979 than it had been earlier in the 1970s;
3. By 1979, Egypt was given more favorable coverage than was Israel, and coverage of Israel was only slightly more favorable than that given Arab states (other than Egypt) and the PLO;
4. For Egypt, Israel, and the PLO the biggest change in television news treatment came from Sadat's trip; for all other Arab states the more minor change that occurred was after the 1973 war.

Taken together these findings indicate that the historic pro-Israeli coverage in US television underwent a remarkable shift during the 1970s. The 1976–77 sample of stories (before Sadat's trip to Jerusalem) had shown 98 percent of those about Egypt to be *un*favorable or neutral.

In sharp contrast, by 1979, a plurality of the 74 news stories about Israel were unfavorable (45 percent), while not a single one of the 33 stories about Egypt were coded unfavorable.

While studies of print media have contended that the 1973 war was a turning point in coverage, these findings point to Sadat's trip to Jerusalem as the critical period for the more dramatic change in the direction of coverage. Again, that change came primarily in reporting stories about Egypt, Palestinians, and Israel and did not seem to extend to Saudi Arabia, Lebanon, Syria, and other Arab states.

A change was even found in coverage of Palestinians and the PLO. While ignored in the 1973 sample, they were the subject of 20 stories in the 1976–77 sample and 49 stories in the 1979 sample. None of the Palestinian stories were positive in the middle period and three-fourths were negative. In 1979, however, the negative proportion was down to 55 percent and 10 percent of the stories (5 out of 49) were actually judged positive toward the PLO. While this still represents unfavorable coverage, it also reflects a substantial change.

The rest of the Arab world did not enjoy such a marked shift in the tone of coverage. In fact, the ratio of favorable to unfavorable stories about Arab states other than Egypt moved in the direction of more unfavorable coverage. In the 1976–77 period, the ratio was 1:2, pro-con; in 1979, the ratio was 1:3, pro-con. While a majority of the stories in all three periods were coded neutral, these Arab states consistently received unfavorable treatment in between one-fourth and one-third of their stories. Only a handful of their stories were favorable.

## COVERAGE OF ARAB AND ISRAELI LEADERS

The preceding discussion concerned coverage given to nations and collectivities rather than individuals. Do these patterns continue in stories that focused on individual leaders? While the smaller number of stories makes the pattern slightly less stable, the overall findings are indeed repeated.

Table 4.2 shows the number and percent of stories about Arab and Israeli leaders that were coded favorable, neutral, and unfavorable for the 1973, 1976–77, and 1979 periods.

Once again the trend in Egyptian coverage is clear. Anwar Sadat and other Egyptian leaders were depicted in a progressively more favorable light. By 1979, all eight of the sample stories about Sadat and company were coded favorable. That Sadat should be treated so favorably lends additional support for the idea that his trip to Israel was a pivotal event.

Also echoing the earlier findings, Israeli leaders, while getting the best coverage of Mideast leaders, in the early period, suffer a relative decline in 1979. Conversely, PLO leaders went from overwhelmingly unfavorable coverage (94 percent) to 62 percent unfavorable in 1979. While the number of relevant stories of the sample was small, no strong trend was found in the treatment of "other Arab leaders," a finding that parallels the earlier data with regard to "other Arab nations."

## IS TELEVISION NEWS BECOMING PRO-ARAB?

Reversing a couple of decades of reporting traditions, Egypt actually appears to have been the recipient of more favorable coverage than was Israel in 1979. Similarly, Palestinians and the PLO made notable gains on network television. These dramatic changes, it should be emphasized, did not extend to other Arab states, and the distinction is important. Since Anwar Sadat traveled to Jerusalem, both Sadat and Egypt have benefited from more uniformly sympathetic coverage. As Sadat voiced continued concern for the Palestinians and made diplomatic appeals on their behalf, and as Palestinians became more skilled in communicating with the media, television news seemed to have evidenced increased recognition and less hostility toward Palestinians and the PLO. That most other Arab states have distanced themselves from Sadat may have reinforced their villainous status and may help account for their continued unfavorable coverage.

## Table 4.1
### Direction of Middle East Coverage During Three Sample Periods
(ABC, CBS, and NBC combined totals)

| | 1973 | | | 1976–77 | | | 1979 | | |
|---|---|---|---|---|---|---|---|---|---|
| | Favorable | Neutral | Unfavorable | Favorable | Neutral | Unfavorable | Favorable | Neutral | Unfavorable |
| Egypt | 10% | 70% | 20% (n=10) | 0% | 83% | 17% (n=6) | 30% | 70% | 0% (n=33) |
| Israel | 22 | 56 | 22 (n=27) | 40 | 58 | 2 (n=43) | 16 | 39 | 45 (n=74) |
| PLO | — | — | — (n=1) | 0 | 25 | 75 (n=20) | 10 | 35 | 55 (n=49) |
| Other Arab States (Syria, Leb., Saudi Arabia, and "Arabs") | 0 | 74 | 26 (n=23) | 14 | 58 | 28 (n=50) | 11 | 57 | 32 (n=47) |

**Table 4.2**
**Direction of Coverage of Middle East Leaders During Three Sample Periods**
(ABC, CBS, and NBC combined totals)

| | 1973 | | | 1976–77 | | | 1979 | | |
|---|---|---|---|---|---|---|---|---|---|
| | Favorable | Neutral | Unfavorable | Favorable | Neutral | Unfavorable | Favorable | Neutral | Unfavorable |
| Egyptian Leaders | 0% | 33% | 67% (n=3) | 50% | 50% | 0% (n=2) | 100% | 0% | 0% (n=8) |
| Israeli Leaders | 17 | 67 | 17 (n=6) | 37 | 50 | 13 (n=16) | 23 | 58 | 19 (n=31) |
| PLO Leaders | — | — | 0 (n=0) | 0 | 6 | 94 (n=18) | 0 | 38 | 62 (n=8) |
| Other Arab Leaders | 0 | 100 | 0 (n=2) | 17 | 50 | 33 (n=6) | 17 | 66 | 17 (n=6) |

It is not clear whether the 1979 coverage was an aberration or a new state of affairs. If the swing merely reflected television's honeymoon with Sadat, and Begin's ineptness with the media, later studies may find a return to more pro-Israeli coverage. If instead the 1979 approach is sustained—with ongoing critical coverage of Israel and highly positive treatment of Egypt and Sadat, although with mixed and negative tones toward the rest of the Arab world—the ramifications for American public opinion will be important to examine. While coverage in 1979 was a long way from being generally pro-Arab, it was a far cry from the pro-Israeli approach of earlier periods.

## REFERENCES

Adams, William and Phillip Heyl. 1981. From Cairo to Kabul on TV News, 1972–1980. In William Adams, ed., *Television Coverage of the Middle East*. Norwood, N.J.: Ablex.

Asi, Morad. 1981. Arabs, Israelis and U.S. Television Networks: A Content Analysis of How ABC, CBS, and NBC Reported the News Between 1970–1979. Ph.D. dissertation, Ohio University.

Bagnied, Magda and Steven Schneider. 1981. Sadat Goes to Jerusalem: Televised Images, Themes, and Agenda. In William Adams, ed., *Television Coverage of the Middle East*. Norwood, N.J.: Ablex.

Budd, Richard W., Lewis Donohew, and Robert K. Thorp. 1967. *Content Analysis of Communications*. New York: Macmillan.

Hofstetter, C. Richard. 1976. *Bias in the News*. Columbus: Ohio State University.

Nasir, Sari J. 1976. *The Arabs and the English*. London: Longman Group Ltd.

Patterson, Thomas E. 1978. Assessing Television Newscasts: Future Directions in Content Analysis. In William Adams and Fay Schreibman, eds., *Television Network News: Issues in Content Research*. Washington, D.C.: School of Public and International Affairs, George Washington University, pp. 177–187.

Perry, Glenn. 1975. Treatment of the Middle East in American High School Textbooks. *Journal of Palestine Studies* 4 (Spring 1975): 46–58.

Suleiman, Michael. 1977. National Stereotypes as Weapons in the Arab-Israeli Conflict. *Journal of Palestine Studies* 3 (Spring 1977): 109–21.

# 5

## ISRAEL IN LEBANON:
## LANGUAGE AND IMAGES OF STORYTELLING

### ITZHAK ROEH

During 1979, Israel's role in the strife-torn region of southern Lebanon became yet another issue in the Palestine Liberation Organization's ongoing battle for international recognition. Israeli military actions in the area and assistance to Lebanese Christians were branded as military expansionism by PLO supporters. While sympathy for the PLO had been growing steadily on the European continent, the United States had resisted the pro-PLO trend. By 1979, however, Americans had begun to exhibit noticeably less tolerance for Israel's involvement on its northern border, and they turned an increasingly attentive ear to PLO interpretations of the Lebanese conflict.

What part was played by American network television news in cultivating this change in public opinion toward Israel and the PLO? What were the messages received by American viewers? How did the media's emphasis on personal tragedy and pathos affect the tenor of coverage? Who were the actors, the heros and villains, featured in US coverage? In what context were the stories portrayed? Was there an emphasis on logical argument or did coverage emotionalize the issues? Did it play on American compassion for the underdog? What kinds of images of people, plots, and destinies did viewers receive?

The unique character of television coverage suggests that heroes, conflicts, and dramatic structures will fit together into an overall pattern. Coverage would probably stress emotionalism, destruction, and pathos, at the expense of a more dispassionate discussion of the issues. In simplistic terms, Israelis may be depicted as aggressors, Palestinians as victims. If TV news is found to dramatize isolated incidents and ignore the larger setting, then changes in American public opinion concerning Israel and the PLO may well have been influenced in part by television's dominant messages.

This study of US television news of Israeli activity in southern Lebanon can address some of these issues related to the formal components of coverage. The underlying assumption of this analysis—an approach that might be termed "structural content analysis"—is that elements of content (or subject matter) and form, distinct as they may be analytically, are in practice interrelated and interdependent. To put it more forcefully: symbolically presented content is conceivable only in terms of its specific form of presentation.

The researcher's painstaking task is first to distinguish among various factors in order to synthesize them, to "dissect" in order to "harmonize." The "whole," that is the entire unit under consideration—"video-texts" in this case—is necessarily a combination of the parts from which it is constructed.[1] Those parts can be described and understood by examining the regularities and patterns that determine the content-form correlations. (Analogously, one can think of the most basic goal of linguistics: the attempt to uncover the structure of language through such regularities as sound-meaning correlations.)

Because our object of observation is television, one obvious question is concerned with the interaction of visual and audial components (see Adams & Schreibman, 1978, pp. 155–69, 139–47, 74). This study will consider the relationship between picture and sound elements after having analyzed separately the implications of the spoken messages. The review of the verbal language explores how it works in various stories and how selected linguistic patterns relate to each other and to the whole unit under consideration.

Using the *Television News Index and Abstracts*, ABC, CBS, and NBC early evening news stories were selected for analysis if they concerned Israeli activity in Lebanon or closely related events. A twenty-two day period from June 25 through August 15 was examined and thirty-six stories were found. With support from the Television and Politics Program of the School of Public and International Affairs of George Washington University, a compiled videotape of these stories was secured from the Vanderbilt Television News Archive. The videotapes were studied at the Communications Institute of the Hebrew University of Jerusalem.

In terms of manifest content, three underlying motifs recur in coverage. (Manifest content is that which can be paraphrased beyond the specifics of presentation, beyond a given structure, beyond latent meanings and connotations.) The three salient motifs that appeared in the unfolding story of Israel in Lebanon were as follows:

---

[1] E.D. Hirsch (1960), not a committed structuralist, emphasizes coherence in his famous essay "Objective Interpretation," where he explores the way in which coherence depends upon context.

First, Israeli military forces attack targets in Lebanese territory, inflicting damage and casualties among both Palestinian and Lebanese civilians.

Second, the United States seems to be tilting toward the PLO, magnifying tension between Israel and the U.S. and creating "a strain," "frictions," and "irritations."

Third, Israel seems to be losing its sources of inner strength that enhance its solidarity and prestige.

In the background were the peace talks with Egypt, with the Palestinian issue comprising a major obstacle to their successful completion. The major focus of the analysis that follows is on the news presentation and development of the first motif—Israeli military actions in Lebanon, their consequences, and sometimes their impetus.

## REITERATING STORIES

Observers and analysts are unavoidably confronted with the self-defeating intricacies of "neutral presentation" as well as with the ever present need to choose among linguistic variations. Even in the most elementary relay of a given content, no author or speaker is free of the necessity to choose words, syntax, and order of presentation. It does make a difference if "friction" and not "dispute" is chosen; "erosion" and not "tilt"; "seems to be losing" and not "losing." Also, it makes a difference to say "Palestinians" and not "PLO," "guerrillas," or "terrorists."

Selecting a story line involves even more complex choices. Such choices belie the "hackneyed maxim that television news 'tells it like it is,'" as Epstein puts in (1973, p. 152). Epstein quotes an NBC producer who instructs his staff that "every news story should have structure and conflict, problem and denouement, rising action and falling action, a beginning, a middle and an end" (p. 153). "In network news," concludes Epstein (p. 175), "the meaning is prescribed by the story line." Epstein echoes European scholars like Barthes (1967) who insists that "facts exist only linguistically as a term in discourse" because "communicating is interpreting" and writing or talking is defining and structuring reality. Barthes links historical discourse, seemingly fact, with fiction, seemingly words (see also Berger & Luckman, 1967).

CBS (6/24):

The pattern is growing familiar: bomb explosion in Israel is followed by an Israeli air attack on Palestinian targets in southern Lebanon. Today it happened again: a bomb went off in a crowded Tel-Aviv bus terminal, and two Arabs who apparently were carrying it were killed. Hours later Israeli planes bombed parts of southern Lebanon and at least twenty people reportedly were killed or wounded.

The concrete news story is skillfully squeezed into a ready-made framework of expectations. These happenings—which must have news value and be somewhat new or unknown—are patterned and familiarized. Today's news story, the announcer implies, is an illustrated proof of a general truth shared by speaker and listeners. As with all storytelling, even surprise and suspense are conceivable only from within a framework of the expected and already known. In this vein, a question as to the assumed differences between fiction and nonfiction, between storytelling and fact reporting, must come to the fore. Is news writing so different from storytelling?

Most journalists have little reluctance to say that they write history, not fiction—that they record facts, true facts, only facts. If the discovery of a pattern through which the-specific-illustrates-the-general is valid, then together with Aristotle we must draw the conclusion that journalists unwittingly write stories no less than they record "true facts of life."[2]

Indeed this pattern does obstinately recur in these newscasts Efforts are made to fit the story to a given frame of expectations, a frame of reference shared by broadcast journalists and their audience. In his *Rhetorics*, Aristotle observes that it is easier to praise citizens of Athens in the ears of citizens of Athens. He also knows that to be understood, one should address an audience in its proper language and use common knowledge, shared associations, and existing values. Similarly, abstractions should follow concrete examples that language can mobilize.

Stories thus tend to constitute specific illustrations of some perceived universal truth. A story may also be somewhat unexpected, but in a way that reaffirms that from which it divorces itself. To arouse surprise or a sense of novelty, a story requires some common knowledge and a shared basis of expectations.

CBS (6/27):
For the first time in five years a confrontation between Israeli and Syrian warplanes [took place in Lebanon].

(Here the new is presented in the context of the old.)

NBC (6/27):
First dogfight between Syrian and Israeli warplanes since 1974 in Lebanon today. In the last five years Syria lost 110 planes while Israel lost three. Israel remains the strongest power in the area.

[2] While defending poetry (storywriting included) from the wrath of Plato, Aristotle makes his distinction between the historian who reports observable incidents and the poet who reports not what has actually happened, but rather that which should have happened. The latter report conveys a "higher," more general kind of truth dealing with human nature and the human condition. Aristotle thus refutes Plato's rejection of poetry in the name of offended truth. The understanding of the nature of news can gain from this well-worn debate. (Also see Robert Darnton, 1975, for some illustration of news writing "under the influence of inherited techniques of storytelling").

(Reaffirmation through an illustration. A theory withstands another empirical test. Old mixed with new information.)

> NBC (7/23):
> Long range artillery from Israel bombarded targets in Lebanon *again* today.

(New news, but not entirely.)

> NBC (7/24):
> Israeli troops *again* raided Lebanon, less than a day after the U.S. demanded to stop such raids.
> NBC (7/29):
> Despite the absence of Begin, the cabinet took a decision he is so well known for.

(Only limited surprise, again.)

> NBC (8/1):
> President Carter in an interview in the *New York Times* is quoted as saying the Palestinian cause is similar to the civil rights movement in the U.S.

The President, to be intelligible, also uses a frame of reference shared with the audience. Arafat knows this too when he addresses the American people through a television interview (CBS, 7/3). Waving his finger with reproach, he says, "You are moved by Vietnamese refugees, but what about 600,000 refugees of *my* people who became homeless by *your* American weapons."

Storytelling is helped when the plot belongs to a family of stories which are linked to existing beliefs and knowledge. The particular story provides the vivid illustration or evolution of the general cluster of stories:

> NBC (8/8):
> "*New* strains, frictions, irritations between the U.S. and Israel"

("New" means "more" here; we are supposed to know of the old ones.)

> ABC (7/23):
> "Once again war planes over Lebanon..."

(We knew they would come again.)

> ABC (7/24):
> "Israel keeps the pressure on Lebanon."
> CBS (8/1):
> "Israel has been hailed as a democracy in the Middle East, but lately there have been charges that the scales of justice were not evenly weighed..."

(Dramatic development and potential conflict; Israel and the U.S. were supposed to share values on democracy and human rights.)

ABC (7/26):

"Overseas: The Middle East is a point of friction *again today* between the U.S. and Israel."

This important principle of newswriting is linking the new with the old. News bears a tension between that which is new and that which we already know. News holds a similar tension between the concrete, here-and-now element and the more abstract and general. Galtung and Ruge (1970) suggest the same dialectics in news; news must at the same time be unexpected yet conform to basic expectations.

Counterpressures of patterning and standardization, on the one hand, and of the deviant and surprising, on the other, create a kind of compromise, a balance that makes stories similar to each other and more readily accepted by audiences. Both pressures, while contrasting, are inherent in the art of storytelling; and they determine in part the sagas of the nightly news.

## REPEATED SYMBOLS AND SIGNS

The subject is the autonomy talks between Egypt and Israel with an American mediator's participation. Words on the screen (NBC, 7/6) read: "The Palestinians." The still, rear-projection picture shows women and children—the helpless, the victims—marching on a road that seems to take them nowhere.

Carter's emissary, Strauss, says something about a breakthrough; and the announcer opens the item by saying, "There was some progress today; the parties agreed on an agenda. . ." Yet, no breakthrough is indicated by the images projected behind the announcer.

If the rhetoric of storytelling includes elements that link the concrete with the general, the rhetoric of the image (Barthes, 1977) does so even more. Key pictures (especially the same often-used stills) that symbolize and signal certain topics in the news appear to need little elaboration. Specific news stories change but the stills are there to stay. They serve further to connect new stories with old truths, stock images, repeated stories, and societal conventions.

An NBC announcer (7/10) starts by saying: "The trouble between Israel and Egypt is the Palestinians." To that verbal "general truth" that helps rhetorically to determine our perception and understanding, a visual message is added. The screen reads "Palestinian talks" and shows the same pictures of helpless women and children. It suggests not only that "Palestinians"are refugees but also that "Palestinian talks" are juxtaposed and perhaps identified with the same women and children.

Another recurrent visual image is the projection of a map of southern Lebanon. Whenever the anchor is talking about Israeli troops or warplanes raiding or attacking, US viewers can be sure to see on all three networks a map of Lebanon with a symbol showing the location of an explosion. This symbol is usually a white or red star that pinpoints the scene of the attack. (A similar combination of stars and maps appear on ABC, 7/22, 7/24, 8/3, 8/15; on CBS, 7/22, 7/24, 3/8; and on NBC, 7/23, 7/24 and 8/3.)

These graphics heighten the message of attackers and attacked, aggressors and victims. A helpless, passive land is shown—usually with little explanation—as having been wounded, scarred, hit. For some reason Israel puts a blot on an otherwise calm map.

The victim motif emerges in other ways as well. When the ABC announcer says (7/23), "Israeli planes again over Lebanon today—State Department condemns the raids on villages in Lebanon," the juxtaposed picture is a destroyed house in a village and then a close-up of a ruined bicycle. The story continues:

Reporter: Eighteen killed and fifteen wounded in the Israeli raid. Israel says she attacked guerrilla concentrations.[3]

Picture: A crying woman helped by two civilians.

Reporter: Lebanon says most casualties are civilians who were picnicking. Some did not find their homes when they came back.

Picture: The same crying woman with the two civilians who are also weeping.

Reporter: The Israeli attacks during the last two months brought about 100,000 refugees in Lebanon.

Picture: The same crying woman.

Let us assume for a moment that the language of the report connotes nothing, suggests no point of view, and "reflects" nothing but the facts. What, in such a case, is the role played by the pictures in the construction of the total message? Clearly the picture questions the validity of the Israeli claim; it supports the Lebanese interpretation; and it contributes to the impression of aggressors versus pathetic victims.

In the last-quoted remark about the impact of the previous two months, the language uses the picture as an illustration of a more general truth. Language and pictures can reinforce each other's claim in the service of a coherent message.

---

[3] Actually, Israeli authorities would never term them "guerrillas." PLO members, as well as members of affiliate organizations, are without exception referred to as "terrorists."

CBS (7/24):

The State Department sharply condemned Israeli raids against Palestinian camps and bases today in Lebanon.

Pictures that follow are of ruined houses, an old Arab man walking around calmly and slowly, and another Arab civilian peacefully riding a donkey. Nothing in the pictures resembles a "base" or Palestinian "camps and bases." Nevertheless, the picture conveys the message of a violent conflict between the strong and weak, the active and passive, the aggressor and victim.

Pictures are not always congruent with the verbal script. In some of these stories, the pictures act in opposition to the text. (See Adams, 1978, pp. 164–68). For example, while Strauss is said "to get things moving" (NBC, 7/10), the film conveys the seemingly unchanging plight of sad Palestinian refugees. Similarly, all three networks (7/11) stressed that Begin and Sadat "failed today to resolve any of their major differences," but the visual images of the two men smiling warmly and being demonstrably friendly seemed to belie this voiceover message. The networks described Begin's reception in Alexandria as "correct" or "reserved," but the viewers were shown a rather enthusiastic reception in the streets of Alexandria.

## AGGRESSOR-VICTIM PATTERNS

To be sure, extra-linguistic reasons may partially account for actors being more or less salient in a news story. Israel's responsibility for its military actions is, as a rule, claimed by a military spokesperson; the active-voice seems only natural. At the same time, terrorists' bombs usually are planted secretly and explode without any obvious actor's intervention; so the passive-voice comes to the fore.

NBC (6/24):

Israeli planes attacked several targets in southern Lebanon, after a bomb exploded in a bus terminal in Tel-Aviv.

Linguistic choices, however, are always there. It is the nature of the final product that is our concern, extra-linguistic phenomena be what they may. The NBC story above could have begun in the beginning. In the beginning there was the bomb.

CBS (6/24):

A bomb went off today in a crowded Tel-Aviv bus terminal, and two Arabs who apparently were carrying it were killed. Hours later Israeli planes bombed parts of southern Lebanon and at least twenty people reportedly were killed or wounded.

In this instance, the reason for the Israeli attack is given; the real world order of events is represented in the story and indicates a cause and effect relationship between the two events. First comes first. Yet, there is repeated more than a tinge of a pathetic mood in the story of the Arabs who "apparently" carried the bomb but were (for sure) "killed."

Some additional reinforcing aspects of the presentation contribute to the same "mood," supporting the strong contrast between "apparently" doing something and consequently being killed. Again a bomb "passively" exploded, whereas Israeli planes "actively" bombed. The link between bomb carrying and being killed in Tel-Aviv is not as obvious as the link between plane bombing and being killed or wounded[4] in Lebanon. And what is more, two casualties in Israel are juxtaposed with the twenty in Lebanon. Even when they appear to be the aggressors, Arabs here are the victims. In presentational terms, from the beginning to the end of this particular story, they are fatalistic victims, not active purposeful figures.

Stereotyped Israeli radio language in such a case would surely announce: "Two terrorists were killed today when trying to plant a bomb in a crowded Tel-Aviv bus terminal." In this account, relationships are presented differently and responsibility is assigned differently. This construction allows little ambiguity regarding the goals, actions, and risks taken by the two people labeled "terrorists." Those killed in this story are no longer pathetic victims. They may be "tragic" in some sense, but this would be an altogether different opera. Israeli attackers may also be tragic actors, but they certainly are not pathetic; tragic actors are at least partly knowledgeable and responsible for their deeds.

In a number of instances, the aggressor-victim structure is reinforced by selected verbal ambivalence. A "language of facts" may be distinguished from "subjective language" that refers not necessarily to reality but to perceptions of reality as expressed by particular speakers.[5] If an authoritative language is associated with one kind of information, while an equivocal language is link with another, then the latter mode of presentation may erode the stature and impact of that information.

NBC (7/22):
Israeli warplanes raided [along] the coast of Lebanon today five towns which Israel calls "terrorist concentrations."

---

[4] "Killed or wounded" is an especially vulgar pattern. It makes a considerable difference whether people are killed or they are wounded, and, as a newscaster myself, I have never used this phrase on the air.

[5] Elsewhere I discuss in some detail the Rhetoric of Objectivity as opposed to that of Subjectivity, especially with regard to news language. Roeh, Katz, Cohen, and Zelizer (1980, pp. 118–22) advocate, from both aesthetic and political points of view, the use of "nonobjective rhetoric" in news parlance. Nonobjective rhetoric, it is speculated, may promote a more intensive perception and better understanding of the news.

The "raid" on "five towns" is presented as a fact of reality. This contrasts with the "subjective language" that implies that while terrorist concentrations might conceiveably exist somewhere "out there," they may well only be a mental construct of one of the parties involved.

Authoritative, undisputed information comes from the network and the reporter, while questionable information is that for which the announcer takes no responsibility. Quoting and emphasizing subjectivity is a common technique in journalism and it will suffice to cite a few illustrations with italics added:

ABC (8/3):
The Israelis *claim* they killed seven PLO people.
ABC (8/7):
Israel *says* it acts for its self defense.
ABC (7/24):
Israel keeps up the pressure on Lebanon...

(so says ABC, but...)

The Israelis *say* the Palestinian guerrillas used it as a base for raids into Israel.

(ABC is not responsible for that information.)

ABC (8/15):
...a tilt in the U.S. attitude...

(says the network.)

Vice Premier Yadin *says* it is a clear violation of the US commitment...

(That much for who says what.)

Another source of ambivalence is the use of vague terms and the special labeling of offensive phenomena.

ABC (8/13):
Strauss wants to see the Palestinians in the talks now.

(Which Palestinians? Does he mean the PLO but wants to avoid this issue?)

NBC (8/8):
Strauss wants Israel to deal with the Palestinians.
CBS (8/5):
American overtures toward Palestinians...
NBC (8/5):
A Palestinian bomb...
ABC (7/22):
"Israel attacks Palestinian bases...

(Bases can be the PLO's, or those of some other affiliate group, but not simply "Palestinian.")

CBS (7/23):
Israeli raids against Palestinian camps and bases...

Camps and bases differ considerably from each other, as do "killed or wounded." Television journalists are not always expected to make such distinctions. The writing of current history with no perspective confuses it all: PLO and Palestinians, refugees and guerrillas, terrorists and civilians, bases and camps.

What makes, for the media at least, Moslems more "progressive" than Arab Christians? Is it that complex of Western self-hate for which some Jews are so famous? Political psychologists might offer an answer. In any event, for Western media, "progress" goes with "left" and with the Moslems in Lebanon, while Christians are either rightists (which is bad) or reactionaries (which is worse).

ABC (7/24):
Israel keeps the pressure on Lebanon. Israeli raiders helped by right-wing Christian militiamen blew up a home in southern Lebanon.

Nothing is more "natural" for the media, it appears, than to use the rhetoric of labeling, of ready-made categories, of commonplace comparisons. All these are rhetorical devices recommended by Aristotle to catch the audience's ear. But such words may confuse and confound the situation in order to make news quickly presentable.

One rhetorical device that almost never appears on television news is what the Russian Formalists term "laying bare the device" (see Erlich, 1969, pp. 63, 190, 248). Laying bare the device is a fundamental expression of irony, of detachment, and perhaps of self-parody; it is a self-reference on the part of a speaker or author that points up the subjective presence of the communicator. This practice contrasts to the usually strict use of "objective rhetoric" on newscasts. Among the thirty-six stories that were analyzed, there was only once in the words of the reporters a clear self-reference that also implied a subjective role or relativity-as-truth. That ABC story (7/6) involves a review of some explicitly personal impressions and views by a reporter on "moods" he sensed in a trip through the Middle East.

A second example originates with Robert Strauss, not with the networks. A CBS reporter said (7/3), "Strauss describes his first mission to Israel as, quote, 'useful, constructive and all those nice words,' unquote." In this little parody, it is Strauss, not the reporter, who takes liberty to lay the device (of his own speech and style) bare. News reporters rarely take such liberties, sticking instead to the code of objective rhetoric.

Although US media operate under the "objective rhetorical" prescription of "letting the facts speak for themselves," the "facts" are subject to many crucial alternative means of presentation through language and images. Like other symbolic and literary objects, news may be studied for its linguistic and presentational forms and constraints; it may be examined for the poetics of news genres.

In the summer of 1979, the stories that flowed from network newsrooms about Israel and southern Lebanon were continuously packaged to fit simplistic, conventional forms and inherited patterns of storytelling. Beyond specific informational details, many of these stories were structured with an implied plot of aggressors versus victims. Active agents of a powerful party were opposed to passive, suffering participants. In this drama the latter group appeared to bear no responsibility for their fate. This pattern was suggested by both the visual and verbal "grammars," and through the interaction of the two. The political and military situation in this part of the world is highly problematic, but some dominant characteristics of television news language have made it even more problematic; or so, at least, it seems. Coverage of destruction and bombing in southern Lebanon was rarely diluted by discussion of the rationale for such activity. American television tended to depict the events as excuses for aggression rather than as retaliation or as preemptive strikes against terrorism.

## REFERENCES

Adams, William and Fay Schreibman. 1978. *Television Network News: Issues in Content Research*. Washington, D.C.: School of Public and International Affairs, George Washington University.

Barthes, Roland. 1970. Historical Discourse. In M. Lane, ed., *Structuralism*. London: Cape.

————· 1977. Rhetoric of the Image. In Roland Barthes, *Image-Music-Text*. New York: Hill & Wang.

Berger, J. and J. Luckmann. 1967. *The Social Construction of Reality*. Garden City, N.Y.: Doubleday.

Darnton, Robert. 1975. Writing News and Telling Stories. *Daedalus* 104 (2): 175–193.

Epstein, Edward J. 1973. *News From Nowhere*. New York: Vintage.

Erlich, Victor. 1969. *Russian Formalism*. The Hague: Mouton.

Galtung, Johan and Mari H. Ruge. 1970. The Structure of Foreign News. In Jeremy Tunstall, ed., *Media Sociology*. London: Constable Press.

Hirsch, E. D. 1967. *Validity in Interpretation*. New Haven, Conn.: Yale University Press.

Roeh, Itzhak; Elihu Katz; Akiba Cohen; and B. Zelizer. 1980. *Almost Midnight: Reforming Late Night News*. Beverly Hills, Ca.: Sage.

# 6

## IMAGES OF SAUDIS AND PALESTINIANS:
## A REVIEW OF MAJOR DOCUMENTARIES

### JACK SHAHEEN

The racism that led to the internment of Japanese-Americans during World War II was created partly by the motion picture industry, which for years typecast Orientals as villains, and partly by the press, especially the newspapers of William Randolph Hearst (see Broek, Barnhart, and Matson, 1954). The "yellow peril" hysteria and the stereotyping which helped produce that myth have retreated into history. The Arab has now become the latest victim of media stereotyping (Ghareeb, 1977). As any television viewer knows, a villain is needed in conflicts that pit good against evil. Today's television villain is often the Arab, simplistically and unfairly portrayed.

Arabs are shown as oil-rich moguls intent on exploiting the American economy, or as faceless terrorists murdering innocent people. These media stereotypes prompted syndicated columnist Nicholas Von Hoffman (1977) to write: "No religious, national, or cultural group has been so massively and consistently villified." Meg Greenfield (1977) has commented: "There is a dehumanizing circular process at work here. The caricature dehumanizes. But it is inspired and made acceptable by an earlier dehumanizing influence, namely, the absence of feeling for who the Arabs are and where they have been."

Only a fraction of the Arab population is oil rich in contrast to television's image. Arabs, like Americans, are both city dwellers and farmers. Some dress in robes, others in the latest Western fashions. Some are light-skinned and others are dark-skinned. There are Arab Jews. There are Arab poets, artists, diplomats, journalists, craftsmen, doctors, and teachers. Yet, prime-time television's picture of the Arab world ignores this diversity and equates Arab with terror (Palestinians) or with oil (Saudis).

In the great expanse of the Arab world, there are over 150 million Arabs. In the United States, two million citizens are of Arab descent; for them the media's anti-Arab bias is an inescapable fact of daily life (see Shaheen, 1980).

Most minorities have come into their own on the television screen. Blacks have graduated from janitorial and servant jobs to become doctors, lawyers, and scientists. Latins are no longer confined to "Frito Bandito" or "Chiquita Banana" roles. American Indians no longer massacre helpless whites and Orientals are no longer shown as shuffling coolies or ruthless villains. Television has discontinued most pejorative characterizations of racial, religious, and ethnic minorities. Arabs however, have been excluded from television's cultural changes. As Hollywood producer Harve Bennett told me: "The Arabs are the last barbarians."

Although television's entertainment image of Arabia has reinforced viewer prejudices, such is not the case with television documentaries. A number of important documentaries have offered other perspectives. Since the mid-1970s, the Middle East has been the subject of several television documentaries and many special news reports on such programs as *CBS Reports*, *60 Minutes*, NBC's *White Paper*, and ABC's *Closeup* series. The Saudis and the Palestinians have been the focus of some of these shows. This report will examine how the Saudis and the Palestinians have been depicted.

Like the producer of television entertainment programs, the documentarist must select topics, people, camera angles, words, and music. But, unlike the entertainment producer, the documentarist is committed not to invent. Instead, the attempt is to capture fragments of reality and arrange them in a meaningful manner. Unlike the producers of the nightly news shows, the documentarist usually has much more time to consider the overall balance and impact of the final news package, more time to conduct interviews and do extensive research, and more time to write and evaluate the script. While newscast stories are typically no more than a couple of minutes long, the documentary offers nearly an hour of air time on one subject. Consequently, the portrayal of these two important Middle Eastern peoples—the Saudis and the Palestinians—on network television documentaries is of special interest.

## SAUDI STEREOTYPES

One *60 Minutes* segment opens with Morley Safer sitting comfortably in the back seat of a Rolls Royce. Next to Safer appears to be an Arab sheik, actually an actor playing the part of a sheik. The Rolls Royce stops in front of a luxury hotel. The driver-actor turns to the sheik-actor and asks: "What shall I do with the car, sir?" "Keep it," says the actor-sheik.

This sequence was omitted from the official CBS transcript of the December 4, 1977, segment entitled "The Arabs Are Coming." (Imagine the reaction had Safer and producer John Tiffin done a show titled "The Jews Are Coming" or "The Blacks are Coming" or "The Indians Are Coming.")

The thesis of this program is that there are lots of Arabs spending lots of money in London. "London's been taken by storm." Safer says the city "has experienced nothing like this invasion." "They come for three or four months," he states, "and they come to buy anything that is not nailed down, plus an awful lot that is."

Safer interviews several prominent men who conduct business with Arabs. Through these interviews the viewer is told that: after an Arab has purchased an English home, "it smells different;" Arabs have rather "garish" tastes in decorating; King Khalid spent $70,000 for flowers during his three-week stay at a London hospital but "no one knows how much was spent on doctors;" and Arabs are "buying up bits and pieces of British history." Safer observes that "people may mock the Arabs behind their backs or be downright racist, but they happily accept their money" and that "in the oil business, it's just all chicken feed."

Safer only interviews one Arab, a young man gambling at a casino. Immediately following the brief interview, he comments: "They're rarely interviewed, because it seems that the Arabs are reserved, formal, stiff-upper-lip kind of people, and the volatile British do not understand them. And so it makes for some confusion."

Safer concludes this enlightening analysis with the statement: "In London, the cobbles echo with the cry to the nation of shopkeepers: 'The Arabs are coming! The Arabs are coming!'"

Similarly, another *60 Minutes* segment—"The 600 Million $ Man"— had exploited the myth that Arabs, especially Saudis, are buying up America. In the January 2, 1977, program tease, Morley Safer remarks that in the US "Arab investment has now passed twenty billion—twenty billion dollars!—and rises about one billion a year." The report goes on to stress the importance of a Saudi Arabian named Khashoggi in Arab trade and investments in the United States. (Khashoggi complains that investments from the Arab world are "colored' and labeled as "Arab money" in a way that German marks or French francs are not.) Shafer never explains that Arab investment in the US remains small in comparison to the investments from other countries (see Chavez, 1980; Thimmesch, 1979).

A slightly different view of the Saudis emerges on an NBC *White Paper* entitled *No More Vietnams...But* with Edwin Newman and Garrick Utley (September 4, 1979). This documentary examined America's dependence on foreign oil, strife in Yemen, Oman's role in guarding the strategic Strait of Hormuz, and Soviet and US military might. Half of the program focused on Saudi Arabia. Warned Edwin Newman: "We must understand the Saudis and their problems quickly."

The theme of the program is that America needs the Saudis and other Arabs only because they have oil. As with Morley Safer's segments, there is a stress on Saudi wealth and few interviews with Saudis.

The report begins with stock footage showing frustrated Americans in gas lines. "Nineteen seventy-nine is the year of the gas line," says Newman. He quotes James Schlesinger, who warned that if the Soviets controlled Middle East oil, that would be the end of the world as we know it.

In Saudi Arabia, correspondent Garrick Utley admits that Amerians know little of the Saudis. Yet, there are only five brief interviews with Saudis. Most of the script is Utley's commentary, such as: "The Saudis could, if they chose to, buy General Motors in 18 weeks, Exxon corporation in 25 weeks, all the stocks on the New York and American stock exchanges in 18 years. Or, for something more modest, Tiffany's in 18 hours."

According to Utley, "It is not easy to get to know the Saudis. Wherever you look there are homes surrounded by walls [visuals show a sequence of walls]. . . concrete veils drawn over private life. . . . There are other veils," says Utley as stills of veiled women appear. "A Saudi woman today receives an education. But there are few places where she can work." Utley does not mention that half of all Saudi doctors are women.

"A woman can't drive a car. . . . Saudi Arabia is still a nation of tribes," continues Utley. A pictorial sequence of shots shows the celebration of a traditional tribal ceremony. There are no scenes with Saudi lawyers in Saudi courtrooms. Islam is the religion of the country, says Utley, but the royal family "uses it" for political purposes.

Utley carefully examines the impact of western technology on Saudi culture. A blond child appears on his father's shoulder carrying a can of Pepsi. A montage of the old and new is shown as new buildings replace traditional dwellings. Crumbling structures give way to modern edifices, implying progress. There are new schools and hospitals; $30 billion is spent annually on basic development projects, notes Utley.

The tidal wave of money has brought not only instant prosperity but traffic jams. Shots of American cars, bumper to bumper on a Saudi street, transcend cultural barriers. A traffic jam is a traffic jam. Dr. Ghazi al-Gosaibi, Saudi Arabia's Minister of Industry, explains that his country is trying to modernize in less than a decade. The danger in such a rapid development is that Islam and technology will sometimes clash.

The major strength of the NBC report comes in the analysis of the technological revolution in Saudi Arabia. Change is taking place at an all too rapid pace. Dr. Al-Gosaibi tells Utley that the work ethic of the West is a good thing to copy. But he hopes the Saudis will avoid copying "some of the negative things of your industrial way of life. . . the destruction of the family. . . the loneliness of people." When they become old, says Al-Gosaibi, "they are thrown into an old age house."

Utley's final commentary summarizes the Saudi dilemma: "The oil which has given such wealth [to the Saudis] is the oil which can destroy their traditions, and eventually the stability of their country upon which we depend so much." He speaks over a montage of the old and new Saudi Arabia—silhouette mosque intercut with neon lights and cars.

It is the internal threat—the influx of foreign workers, the clash of cultures, the absence of Saudi participation in the Middle East peace negotiations—that may precipitate a crisis. In an emergency, the Saudis rely on American military support. They have ample tanks and planes, including the American F-15's. The nation has become the "world's largest defense spender." But Utley points out that in spite of its growing military presence, "Saudi Arabia does not have an army strong enough or large enough to defend itself."

"We are commited to defend Saudi Arabia's oil and to protect the Royal Family against domestic unrest or a military coup," says the correspondent. Unlike Iran, there is no human rights issue in Saudi Arabia. Former Ambassador to Saudi Arabia, James Aikens, explains to Utley: "There are some people who are dissatisfied with social progress. But people are not being arrested, they're not being tortured, they don't disappear." Adds Aikens, "People don't make revolutions because women can't drive cars. They make revolutions because their sons are being murdered by the official police. This doesn't happen in Saudi Arabia."

This *White Paper* neglects the Soviet role in the region. Little is said about the possibilities of the Saudis and other Gulf nations doing business with the Russians out of frustration with US Middle East policy or because of the threat of Soviet force. The Saudi Arabian segment is noteworthy because a few Saudi spokesmen offer insightful opinions about the problems facing their nations.

A negative attitude toward the Saudis, however, is prevalent throughout the NBC report. Utley says, "the United States has been forced into a new relationship. . . with a country and a region with which it has no cultural ties, no longstanding political partnership. A relationship which has one common denominator—oil. They have it. We need it." He repeats the statement, "Although we may not like it, we need their oil."

The song "Food for Crude" is played, and the familiar scenes of gas lines with angry motorists in the United States are shown as Utley comments about Ameria's frustrations at the gas pumps. He implies the Saudis are to blame. Scenes of derricks and natural gas flames appear as Utley explains: "Here are the oil installations at work, built by Americans, still run largely under American supervision and which in the case of war would have to be defended by the United States." Americans are the largest Western presence in Saudi Arabia—35 thousand. He then repeats the scenario voiced by former presidential advisor Stuart Eizenstat who publicly urged President Carter to blame the Arabs for America's inflation problems. "An American might ask himself," concludes Utley, "why doesn't the United States simply help itself to some more oil? Or to put it bluntly: why don't we take it?" Utley's closing commentary actually suggests a takeover of Saudi oil fields by American soldiers.

## ANOTHER VIEW OF THE SAUDIS

The Saudis, a CBS Special Report, was telecast on October 21, 1980. The ratings were not very high; it was scheduled opposite the sixth game of the World Series—the highest-rated series game ever. Producer Maurice Murad and correspondent Ed Bradley offer viewers a comprehensive view of Saudi society. The news documentary provides the background necessary to understand the contrasts and contradictions of Saudi Arabian life. Bradley ascertains, after interviewing over a dozen Saudis ranging from women in college to foreign ministers, that Saudi Arabia does not fit the stereotype of camel-riding tribal chieftans who practice oil blackmail and have harems. Nor is it the land of Rudolph Valentino's The Sheik. He suggests that it is a progressive, religious, yet vulnerable nation with important ties to the United States.

The changing nature of Saudi society, its special relationship with the United States, the vulnerabilities of its vast supplies of oil, and the temporal and spiritual leadership—the Royal Family and the Moslem faith—are closely examined. There are no cursory analyses of complex issues.

The 1980 war between Iran and Iraq caused apprehension in the West, and with good reason. The oil fields of Saudi Arabia, just 400 miles from the conflict, were practically defenseless. Bradley contends that if Saudi oil fields were threatened, American troops would probably be called in to defend, not take over, the nation. "It is impossible to overestimate Saudi Arabia's importance to the West,' says Bradley. Their 750 oil wells supply 8 percent of the US's oil, 40 percent of France's, 35 percent of Italy's, and 25 percent of Japan's.

Bradley asks, "Who are the Saudis?" He traces the nation's history, beginning in 1932 when Bedouin tribes became united under the House of Saud, and outlines the development of Saudi Arabia up to the November 1979 attack by religious fundamentalists on the Holy Mosque of Mecca. As for historical monuments, Bradley says, "There is not much left of old Arabia." Today there is a $450 billion building boom. The Saudis now face the conflict of a society embracing modernization while retaining its orthodox ways.

Minister of Industry Ghazi al-Gosaibi believes the Saudi government "is not working against the desires of the people." He contends they want the people to keep their value systems—to make certain the spiritual side does not change. The Minister admits "the material way of life" is being sold to people, and that there are some "who are wheeler-dealers." Saudi Arabia "is not an extension of paradise."

Bradley shows Saudi Arabia as a different society, not necessarily better or worse. He looks at the Saudi system of justice, the Majlis. Every prince and minister in the kingdom holds morning court; people from all over the provinces are given opportunities to seek favors or protest injustices. In Saudi's open courts, says Majahid Al Sawwaf, a religious scholar, "any defendant, any claimant could come to the court without a lawyer. Most of the people would come. . . by themselves." He tells Bradley that "appeals are allowed and procedures followed." For fifteen centuries the Saudis have been ruling according to Islamic law. Referring to some complex civil laws that have developed over the centuries, Bradley notes that the *Koran*, like the US Constitution, is adaptable to changing times.

The documentary is respectful of Islam. The viewer sees Saudis praying alone, or in a crowded mosque, or in a country field, by a tent. The popular stereotype of the Islamic Saudi as a religious fanatic has unfortunately made outsiders "quick to conclude that Saudi Arabia is ripe for revolution." says Oil Minister Sheik Ahmed Zaki Yamani.

The program also indicates that many Saudis shop at the local Safeway. One supermarket scene reveals that Safeways in Saudi Arabia are like those in the United States, from shopping carts to manager's specials. The only difference is the clothing many of the people wear: men wear robes; the women are in black.

Another segment concerns a young government official, Faisal Al-Bashir, who was educated in the United States. He explains to correspondent Bradley that, although he "loved education," he was once considered by the standards of his tribe to be "one of the biggest failures they ever met." Bashir understood their thinking—he was expected to be their leader. It was a special community, says Bashir, where you feel "everyone is your cousin or a brother or a relative. . . . You feel together." He explains to Bradley the beauty and harshness of desert life and the impact of the quiet peace that prevails; it is a peace that he seldom experiences in his new surroundings.

Usually, the technological revolution is measured in material terms of traffic jams and skyscrapers rather than in human terms. Here—perhaps for the first time in a television program—a young Saudi was given the opportunity to express his feelings about the impact of progress on his family and his life.

Bradley continues to elicit Saudi self-expression. He asks women how they feel about not being allowed to drive a car and about men being permitted more than one wife while they can have only one husband. He speaks with students at the oldest Saudi school for women. They are not veiled and, for the first time, young, educated Saudi women are shown on screen playing volleyball, joking, and studying. "No one we spoke with wanted change at the expense of their traditions.... They defended the foundations of their culture," observes Bradley. Unlike NBC's Garrick Utley and CBS's Morley Safer, Bradley takes time to talk with Saudi people. Viewers hear firsthand Saudi opinions on Saudi society.

Most of the young women Bradley interviews have studied and travelled in the United States. They intend to become doctors, biologists, and teachers. Their teacher, Madame Rouchdy, maintains that there is nothing wrong with living in a sexually segregated society, that she and other women are protected, and that it is unfortunate that in the West a segregated society is not acceptable. She asks Bradley, "Why should you always look upon whatever is different from your society as wrong?"

US Ambassador John West tells Bradley that because there is unrest in the Middle East and because the Palestinian problem has not yet been solved he believes that Saudi Arabia, traditionally a moderate in OPEC, may one day use the oil weapon. Saudi Arabian Foreign Minister Prince Saud Al Faisal explains: "The Middle East is not unstable... because Saudi Arabia has large resources of oil. It is because Israel occupies Arab territories and drives the Palestinians out of their homeland." Notes Bradley: "There are over 50 thousand Palestinians working in Saudi Arabia" and they are a constant reminder to the Saudis "of the unsettled issue of the Palestinian homeland."

"The Saudis are now the largest purchaser of American military hardware and services in the world," says Bradley. Yet Ambassador West fears the oil fields, containing 30 to 35 percent of the known oil resources in the world are not easy to defend. The camera shows scenes of the Saudi Army (75,000 men in the armed forces) in training. As to the Russian threat, when and if the Soviets need oil they may be able to take it, not only from Saudi Arabia but from nearby Gulf nations. Notes Bradley, "It would take at least three weeks before a major US strike force could be put down on Saudi soil."

Several unresolved and complex issues cloud American-Saudi relations. Saudis question whether the United States would defend them if there were internal strife or if the Soviets were to attack. They are confused by the US position on a Palestinian homeland or state. Conversely, Americans question whether Saudi oil will continue to flow west, as long as the Palestinian issue remains unsettled. Will Saudi Arabia continue to be a "moderate" in OPEC? And, should American troops defend Saudi soil if the oil fields were to be attacked?

These issues and America's special relationship with Saudi Arabia "will be sorely tested in the months and years to come," concludes Bradley. As he speaks the camera focuses on scenes of Saudi families picnicing on the beach and kids playing soccer between modern buildings. These scenes and others have begun to humanize the image of the Saudis. They contribute to a well-balanced and probing documentary by correspondent Bradley and producer Murad that offers timely insights and explores complex questions without resorting to stereotypes.

## PALESTINIAN IMAGES

Television's stereotypical presentation of the Palestinians was epitomized by a May 19, 1974 segment of *60 Minutes* entitled "The Palestinians." A Palestinian mother is shown flaunting a gun, saying, "The gun will always be with us, always, always." Yassir Arafat appears disheveled and unshaven, and the camera focuses closely on his mouth. Palestinians are portrayed as radical, trigger-happy terrorists. Film footage shows the tragic results of Palestinian raids at Maalot and Quarat Shemona. In "balancing" the Palestinian attacks, an Israeli raid on Beirut, Lebanon, is discussed as retaliation in response to atrocities. No footage is shown of Lebanese or Palestinian casualties resulting from the Israeli raids.

The *60 Minutes* segment ignores the plight of the 3.5 million Palestinian refugees scattered throughout the world. No insight is offered as to who the Palestinians are. Palestinian men, women, and children are pictured as fanatic warmongers. The camera shows a child in an army training camp, and a mother wielding a gun and swearing vengeance. As projected in *60 Minutes*, all Palestinians are terrorists.

In contrast to the *60 Minutes* segment, Howard Stringer's CBS documentary, *The Palestinians* (June 15, 1974), provides an altogether different view of the Palestinians, including the minority who are "terrorists." In the film, correspondent Bill McLaughlin uses neither the terms "terrorists" nor "freedom fighters;" they are referred to as "guerrillas." (Guerrilla comes from the word for war, *guerra*, and is generally taken to mean unconventional warfare.)

Stringer's documentary won the Overseas Press Club award for the best documentary on foreign affairs in 1977. The thesis of the documentary is that "there can be no peace in the Middle East before there is peace between the Palestinians and the Israelis." The initial scenes show Palestinians firing at one another at a training camp. "That's live ammunition they're firing," says McLaughlin. He then explains that the "extreme fringe" of the Palestinians caused the massacre at Maalot. Adds McLaughlin: "These are violent men who can sometimes say frightening things, sometimes reasonable things. They were raised to die for Palestine."

Following his observations of Palestinian guerrillas in Lebanon, they are seen under fire as well as enjoying a traditional song. McLaughlin comments: "They are fighting for an impossible cause: a socialist Palestine made up of Arabs and Jews. All the guerrillas have in common," he says, "is a claim to the same land and a readiness to shake hands with the devil if he'd show them the way home."

The problem in the Middle East is that the promised land has been "promised to two different people at the same time." "Whose promised land?" asks McLaughlin. The Arabs say that history promised Palestine to the Palestinians, he explains, while the Israelis believe God promised Israel to them.

A montage of stock footage depicting the history of the land appears as McLaughlin traces the beginning of the conflict, citing the Balfour statement and the persecuted, homeless Jews of Nazi Germany. Scenes of the early Palestinian refugee camps resulting from the 1948 and 1967 wars are shown. A Palestinian mother comforts her frightened child while McLaughlin explains that it is the Palestinians, "ignored by the West and used by the East," who have been the consistent loser in the four wars fought in their name during this century. As the montage concludes, one has sympathy with both Palestinian and Jew.

In Lebanon, McLaughlin visits one of the many refugee camps and speaks with members of the Yamani family. The son, Maher Yamani, had been jailed in Athens for attacking an El Al plane. He tells McLaughlin that it is wrong to kill Israeli civilians. He says that he and most Palestinian guerrillas are concerned with attacking only military targets. Maher's parents promise that Palestinians will continue to fight. Waving a pistol, Mr. Yamani exclaims that "we Palestinians cannot accept a piece of our own land as charity from another country."

McLaughlin interviews other Palestinians, including members of the commercial elite and the middle class. In Beirut he talks with a civil engineer who would willingly give up his wealth to live in Palestine. He wants to live and develop land there, as he has done in other Arab lands.

The Costandi family are middle-class Palestinians in Lebanon. They tell McLaughlin that there is violence now because the world ignored the Palestinian refugees for nearly twenty-five years. Violet Costandi belives that she and others can live with the Jews. "Yes, we can live together," she says. To her, Palestine is home: "I was born there; I belong there." The interview with the Costandi family shows Americans that there are educated, peace-loving Palestinians.

Elias Frej, mayor of occupied Bethlehem, is also interviewed. Frej advocates an independent Palestinian state on the West Bank, saying, "I announce that we accept and recognize the existence of Israel. But I ask Israel to accept our existence here."

McLaughlin questions Frej as to whether a Palestinian state on the West Bank would actually bring peace. Perhaps some Palestinians would not be satisfied and want "to destroy Israel." Replies Frej, "If you find a Palestinian who says he wants to destroy Israel, he's a foolish man. Israel is a fact. Israel is here to stay."

Concerning the Israeli presence, McLaughlin asks, "What's the Israeli occupation like?" (At the time of the telecast in 1974 there were only 17 Israeli settlements on the West Bank.) "It is an occupation," Frej replies, "like any occupation."

Scenes at a training camp in Lebanon show Palestinians completing a six-month basic training course. McLaughlin documents that they appear, on the surface, a formidable force. But they have no planes, no artillery. "If the guerrillas had a home," he says, "there would be no reason to fight."

McLaughlin interviews Yassir Arafat, who concurs with Mayor Frej, the Palestinian civil engineer, and the Costandi family—he would accept a Palestinian state on the West Bank. Arafat tells McLaughlin that if the Israelis withdraw from the West Bank he will establish a Palestinian state. "We want to live with the Jews," he says.

The conclusion of Stringer's documentary presents Palestinian guerrillas at play as they dance to an Arabic folk song. They are, for the moment, at peace. The camera pulls back to show the beauty of Lebanon's countryside. Says McLaughlin: "Their promised land has yet to be delivered."

Producer Howard Stringer, in a personal interview, said, "Before I made the film about the Palestinians, people said I was going to perpetuate the stereotype." "I think where television has failed," he explained, is that "it doesn't do a great deal of current affairs programming, it hasn't done enough of in-depth news documentaries to correct stereotypes; hour-long documentaries should be stepping into the breach." Stringer added: "I think we've misunderstood the Arab world pretty consistently. . . . Members of the Lebanese government couldn't believe the film was actually shown on network television. They didn't anticipate a program that would give credence to some of the Palestinian aspirations." Stringer emphasized he had no trouble from the network in the conception or production of the film. Then vice president of CBS News, Bill Leonard, approached Stringer on doing a documentary on the Arab world. "It was my idea to do something on the Palestinians," said Stringer. "Believe me, I never had any pressure on that broadcast."

His documentary was unusual for 1974 in at least suggesting that a rationale existed for the idea of a West Bank state. An Arab is quoted as saying he would live on a rooftop in Jerico if it meant the formation of a Palestinian state on the West Bank. Stringer contended that the Israelis on the West Bank, whether they liked it or not, had the role of an army of occupation, a role that would breed resentment and would one day have to be resolved. With a concealed camera, he showed Israelis dismantling a home of a suspected Arab terrorist.

"I worked very hard to show that Arabs were not all sheiks," Stringer said. "There are middle-class and wealthy Palestinians." The 1974 program documents both Israeli and Palestinians points of view, and presents a complex and diverse picture instead of the old Palestinian stereotypes. The documentary does not propose any simple solution and does not offer a villain; it does help explain precisely why the prospects for a peaceful settlement seem so remote and why the Palestinian cause is unlikely to disappear.

## PALESTINIAN TERROR

Another major television documentary about Palestinians was Malcolm Clarke's *Terror in the Promised Land*, broadcast October 30, 1978 on ABC. Like Howard Stringer, Malcolm Clarke is an Englishman who produced, wrote, and directed the documentary. Clarke's documentary gives a rare sympathetic view of Palestinian guerrillas and attempts to explain what motivates them to sacrifice their lives for a land their friends and families had to leave decades ago.

The film is seen through the eyes of young Palestinians—the youngest is sixteen—who volunteer for suicide squads. They express their mission:

> We go on suicidal missions because we have a cause and a principle and a land.
> Better to die in one's own land than outside of it.
> We are happy because I know if I go, there will be others who follow.

Producer-director Malcolm Clarke humanizes Palestinian guerrillas, previously seen primarily as gun-wielding fanatics. The ABC production unit spent weeks in the Middle East seeking out certain Palestinians, trying to understand why they had chosen to sacrifice their lives. The documentary begins with three young Palestinians appearing in a "home movie." They appear innocent. While they smile, the camera cuts to an explosion of a building. Inside, the three youths, along with their Israeli captives, are blown to pieces.

Viewers are shown a "martyr's cemetery" in Beirut. Photographs are neatly placed above the graves of those men who sacrificed themselves for "the cause." Narrator Frank Reynolds explains: "The men knew they were going to die, and also knew they would never be forgotten." Next the ABC unit captures yet another photo session of a suicide squad—freeze-framed shots of human innocence and grief. When their mission ends, they, too, may enter the special cemetery.

In Beirut, Mustafa Zein, a Lebanese businessman who supports the Palestinian cause, asks why it is so hard, in the West, to understand the Palestinian need to regain his identity in his own land. Zein says that anyone of the Jewish faith coming from Russia or the United States "automatically has the right to settle in Israel and to have a passport." He wants to know "why people expect the Palestinians to be less patriotic than the Israelis." Following his comments, there is film footage of Hitler's holocaust. Millions of Jews had been slaughtered, and the survivors wanted their own state. Reynolds then documents the terror—Jewish and Arab—that took place in Palestine before and during 1948. The destruction of the King David hotel in 1947 is shown, although Reynolds does not mention that Prime Minister Begin was then a leader of Irgun, the Jewish group responsible for the hotel explosion and deaths.

Reynolds says: "There is no dispute. Palestinians had lived here for centuries in the land which is now the state of Israel." Scenes of Palestinians beginning their exile in 1948 are matched with shots of today's refugees camps. There are pastoral scenes of a peaceful land. An Arab farmer, alone with his flock, suggests peace is possible.

Another compelling segment in *Terror* has Anna Kanafani, the widow of Ghassan Kanafani, a Palestinian intellectual, describing the assassination of her husband. Mrs. Kanafani, who teaches at a refugee camp, says that, in addition to her husband, other Palestinian civilian intellectuals were assassinated by Israelis. Narrator Reynolds then lists Palestinian officials killed by Israeli raids or by Israeli agents since Kanafani's assassination. Framed in dark colors, the photographs of ten Palestinian leaders appear on the sceen.

The tragedy of *Terror* is revealed in the faces of children making toy grenades in school and being taught to dance and sing about a land they have never seen. The innocence of childhood is transferred to the reality of warfare as the camera cuts from a school to barbed wire. An eleven-year old receives rigorous training in a refugee camp. One day he may be a guerrilla, perhaps a member of a suicide squad.

The documentary also gives credence to the accusation that Israel has tortured Palestinians. A young Palestinian student, Khalid Rubo, describes how he was severely beaten by Israelis. As he speaks, photographs of his badly bruised body appear. An American Red Cross official confirms the torture of some Palestinians in Israeli prisons. The official, however, shared his concern with the US Department of State. "To do that without authorization was contrary to Red Cross policy," states Reynolds, "and the Red Cross official was dismissed."

Israeli settlements on Arab land are discussed. In an interview with Rannon Weitz, director of the Jewish National Fund, Weitz acknowledges that the villages he planned and built are on the land used previously by Arabs, and that the Jews use Arab land for their survival. "The problem," Weitz declares, "is a clash between two justices. And the answer for such a situation is a painful compromise. There is no escape from that."

*Terror* concludes as it began, with the death of a young Palestinian. As narrator Reynolds says, he is "a victim as well as a perpetrator of terror in the promised land, the land of Moses, Mohammed, and Jesus."

Most television critics considered *Terror* to be good broadcast journalism. In *New Yorker* magazine, Michael Arlen wrote (1979): "The ABC documentary showed us more about the Palestinians in fifty-seven minutes than most American news organizations, large or small, have printed or televised in the past dozen years—and showed it with an uncommon mixture of judgment and perspective." Arlen contended that the program "went after a difficult and controversial subject and communicated it with clarity and a respect for history as well as for human feelings."

As Arlen noted, the documentary was not commercially sponsored. Instead, public service announcements were presented for the United Way, the American Lung Association, the National Cancer Institute, the Soil Conservation Service, the International Association of Police, and the Department of Health, Education, and Welfare. All paid commercials were removed, said a network spokeswoman, because the six regular documentary series sponsors were not given sufficient notice of the controversial nature of the program.

The spokeswoman told United Press International that the program attracted three thousand protest calls to ABC stations around the country and that half the calls came in before the program started. She said many of the callers read prepared statements, and some admitted they were told by others to call.

Karl Meyer, *Saturday Review's* television critic, considered *Terror* to be a troubling documentary. Meyer did not question the honest intentions of executive producer Pamela Hill or writer-producer Clarke. "Their professed aim," wrote Meyer (1979), "was to show the human side of the face of the terrorists, and to present the PLO perception of the tangled Arab-Israeli conflict."

Meyer contended that "at every point, the documentary was flawed by its one-sided perspective. . . . A comparison was offered between the terrorist attacks of the PLO and of the Stern Gang and Irgun during the era of British rule in Palestine," noted Meyer, "but without allusion to the important distinction that in nearly all cases, the targets of Jewish terrorism were military and political."

Meyer suggested that ABC should have had a "prescreening before a panel of private citizens with expertise on the subject. . ." "I am told," he said, "that the network did solicit the opinions of a single academic authority on the Middle East, but he happened to be a Columbia professor whom Jewish organizations regard as pro-Arab."

In New York, producer-writer Malcolm Clarke praised the work of the ABC News *Closeup* unit. Clarke told me he received no interference from the network, but that the film had to be locked in a safe every night. "We took the film off the benches and out of the cans, off the machines and locked it up," he said. Because of death threats made against his life and others at ABC, a private security agency was paid by the network to open mail addressed to members of the production team.

Clarke said, "The documentary unit at ABC was very brave to put *Terror* on because there was a lot of pressure." He expressed the highest regard for his executive producer, Pamela Hill, because she was so courageous "in fighting some of the hysterical opposition that came from the outside."

I asked Clarke what he had accomplished with *Terror*. He replied:

> I'm proud it got on the air. I'm proud because the film showed the human face of the Palestinians fighting a cause they believe in. It addressed issues that were fresh and it addressed them honestly. In the past, with some notable exceptions [Clarke mentions the 1974 Howard Stringer documentary] the Palestinians have not been unmasked. Up till now no one has confronted the reality that, face to face, the "terrorist" is a sixteen-year old kid from a refugee camp. That's frightening— when you realize that the kid is only sixteen and that he may never be seventeen, because he believes in something.

## THE CONTRIBUTION OF MIDDLE EAST DOCUMENTARIES

The documentaries discussed in this essay attempt, with varying degrees of success, to explain to Americans the politics and cultures of quite different societies. Such programs help to counteract the tendency to reject, without trying to understand, that which is different. As Howard Stringer said, "If people don't want to be like us [Westerners], we don't understand them." He remarked that "We liked the Shah because he was Americanizing, because he wanted to be like us. Americans have always tended to prefer people that try very hard to Americanize themselves."

That tendency did emerge somewhat in the NBC *White Paper*, although it was much less evident in the other major documentaries discussed here. While the NBC program probed the problems of modernization, there were few interviews with Saudis; instead, correspondent Garrick Utley offered sometimes unfounded generalizations about Saudi society. Utley's impressions of Saudis' "concrete walls drawn over private lives" like their "homes surrounded by walls" never quite descend to the level of sociological and political analysis offered by Marvin Kalb when he observed on a CBS special report (March 25, 1975) that he was not surprised by King Faisal's assassination because in Riyadh he had a clear "feeling" that "you knew it was an environment for plotters." Kalb had said, "People were walking around and there was the—the constant shifting of eyes."

In contrast, CBS's *The Saudi's* destroys the myth of the oil-rich moguls with exploited harems. There are numerous interviews with the people of Saudi Arabia, not merely with a few government representatives. For example, bright and articulate Saudi women, without veils, were interviewed and expressed approval of the Islamic traditions of their country. Viewers were allowed to form some of their own perceptions of Saudis, rather than having to rely entirely on a commentator's judgments.

ABC's *Terror in the Promised Land* and CBS's *The Palestinians* provided contrasting yet realistic protraits of Palestinians. Producer Clarke explores the motivations for the seemingly senseless suicides of youth. Unless there is soon peace, many more children of *Terror* will one day find peace only in a martyr's cemetery. Producer Stringer captures the deepest feelings of exiled Palestinians, those in the prosperous middle and upper classes as well as those engaged in combat. Palestinians with education and financial security share one key trait with the young guerrillas—they yearn for a homeland.

It is not claimed that these documentaries greatly influenced public opinion. They did, however, present an alternative and more balanced perspective that contrasts with the greedy oil sheik images seen in many entertainment shows. They offered some antidote to such stereotyping. Otherwise, as Walter Lippman pointed out, stereotyping tends to be self-perpetuating "pictures in our heads."

The cultures of the Middle East are easily caricatured for the purposes of Hollywood and prime-time television. The Arab peoples are not easily explained in quick two-minute network news stories. Consequently, documentaries have provided important opportunities for more thorough and more accurate examinations of Arab nations.

## REFERENCES

Arlen, Michael J. 1979. ABC Visits the PLO; the Sponsors Stay Home. *New Yorker*, November 13, 1979.

Broek, Jacobus ten, Edward N. Barnhart, and Floyd W. Matson. 1954. *Prejudice, War, and the Constitution*. Berkeley: University of California Press.

Chavez, Linda. 1980. Kuwait Makes Bid. *Los Angeles Times*, July 15, 1980.

Ghareeb, Edmund. 1977. *Split Vision: Arab Portrayal in the American Mass Media*. Washington, D.C.: Institute of Middle Eastern/North African Affairs.

Greenfield, Meg. 1977. Our Ugly Arab Complex. *Newsweek*, December 5, 1977, p. 110.

Meyer, Karl. 1979. Supping with the Devil. *Saturday Review*, February 3, 1979, p. 33.

Shaheen, Jack. 1980. The Arab Stereotype on Television. *The Link* (published by Americans for Middle East Understanding, 475 Riverside Drive, New York, N.Y.), April/May, 1980.

Timmesch, Nick. 1979. Arabs: The Latest Scapegoats. *Washington Post*, February 9, 1979.

Von Hoffman, Nicholas. Israeli Torture: Disturbing London Times Report. *Washington Post*, July 1, 1977.

## INTERVIEWS

Harve Bennett, personal interview, Los Angeles, July 7, 1980.

Malcolm Clarke, personal interview, New York City, September 11, 1980.

Howard Stringer, personal interview, New York City, September 9, 1980.

# 7

## THE INVASION OF AFGHANISTAN: DOMESTIC VS. FOREIGN STORIES

### MONTAGUE KERN

Foreign affairs coverage has two dimensions: the foreign story that deals with events abroad and the domestic story that concerns the United States' role and reaction to world events. The first concentrates on interpretation of events by foreign participants; the latter focuses on domestic parties with diverse interests, notably the president and the administration, other political figures, and affected interest groups.

This study will compare these two dimensions of foreign affairs coverage as made evident in a major story involving the Soviet invasion of Afganistan and the United States response. The analysis focuses on the one-month period begining with the first rumors of troop movements on December 21, 1979, through the Iowa precinct caucuses on January 21, 1980, a significant test for critics of the president's foreign policy. It will examine network television coverage of the Soviets, our allies, domestic political figures, interests groups and, not least, President Jimmy Carter, who declared the invasion the greatest crisis since World War II and began a military buildup in the Persian Gulf. Did different standards of reporting apply? How did foreign and domestic coverage interrelate? Did the presidential bias of television mean that the real story of Afghanistan was not so much in the events abroad as in the additional boost given Carter's presidency, which had been steadily losing public support before the Iranian crisis erupted in early November, 1979?

In searching for answers to these questions, content analysis was undertaken involving all stories dealing with both domestic and foreign aspects of the Afghan story between December 21, 1979, and January 21, 1980. A total of sixty-two stories on NBC and sixty on CBS evening news were identified using Vanderbilt's *Television News Index and Abstracts*. These stories totalled about three hours on each network during this one-month period. Using facilities of the TV News Study Center at George Washington University, the videotapes loaned from the Vanderbilt Archive were coded for time, date, topic, and dominant visual details of their 239 cut-to-cut segments. Only segments relating to the Afghan crisis were used from multifaceted campaign stories.

These basic units of analysis were further broken down into the time and position of every source within each story segment quoted either directly or by the newscaster. A total of 223 entries involving 109 different domestic and foreign sources were tallied. Of the three hours total time consumed by the Afghan story on each network, approximately 53 percent was devoted to these source statements by CBS and 40 percent by NBC. (See Table 7.1.) Given the importance of sources, a close analysis of quoting patterns seemed useful in order to determine which foreign and domestic actors were quoted and how they were quoted.

An additional variable was analyzed in order to answer the question of how sources were quoted; this variable concerned newscaster inference in the other portions of the news stories. Did the newscaster introduce or follow a source with a comment which supported, was neutral, or was negative toward the views of the source? Most studies dealing more generally with this issue have found a great deal of neutrality in relation to domestic institutions and political candidates (e.g., Hofstetter, 1976; Robinson & Appel, 1979). Does this hold true when applied specifically to newscaster presentations of sources quoted on highly emotional foreign policy issues during an election campaign?

### Table 7.1
### Afghanistan on the TV News Agenda

|  | NBC | CBS |
|---|---|---|
| Total stories* | 62 | 60 |
| Minutes per day (32 days) | 5.5 | 5.6 |
| Average minutes per story | 2.9 | 3 |
| Days the lead story | 13 | 16 |
| Total segments* | 123 | 116 |
| Average minutes per segment | 1.4 | 1.6 |
| TOTAL MINUTES | 176.9 | 180 |
| TIME IN SOURCES | 71 minutes, 24 seconds (40%) | 95 minutes, 26 seconds (53%) |

* Stories are defined as the separate stories listed in Vanderbilt's *Television News Index and Abstracts;* an evening news "story" on one general subject may be broken down into segments, with each segment having a different locale and reporter. (December 21, 1979–January 21, 1980.)

The crisis selected was indeed highly emotional, although perhaps less so than the more prolonged Berlin crisis of 1961, which similarly led to a change in strategic policy and a military buildup. Walter Cronkite expressed the climate as of January 18: that in the past few days, rumors of Soviet forces moving to the Yugoslav or Iranian borders and reports of Chinese arms for the rebels and of Soviet, British, and American naval forces to the Middle East "fed by Administration sources in Washington," have led to a "rumble of war talk frighteningly reminiscent of the days that preceded World Wars I and II . . . but today the State Department moved to dampen the alarm."

The Afghan invasion received extraordinary treatment during the period under study. Each of the two networks devoted an average of five minutes per day to the issue, an average which includes the seven-day period before December 28, after which the crisis really got under way. On some nights, coverage averaged fifteen minutes per network. The Afghan story was given the lead position on nearly half of the days during the month-long period (see Table 7.1). When the story segments were categorized by topic, great similarities were also found between the networks. Over half of the segments on both networks dealt with foreign aspects of the Afghan story (see Table 7.2).

Of the American sources, 38 percent on CBS and 44 percent on NBC were United States official sources—figures which approximate quite closely the use of official sources found in a study of front page newspaper sources during three other foreign crises (Kern, 1979): the Laotian buildup in 1961 (43 percent), the Berlin crisis in 1961 (38 percent), and the Cuban missile crisis in 1962 (40 percent). The main difference in the Afghan invasion is

Table 7.2
Subjects of Story Segments

|  | NBC | % | CBS | % |
|---|---|---|---|---|
| **Foreign Events** | | | | |
| Soviet action | 29 | 23.5 | 22 | 19.0 |
| Afghans (Karmal Gov't.) | 10 | 8.1 | 15 | 12.9 |
| M.E. & SW Asia response | 9 | 7.3 | 7 | 6.0 |
| Afghans (Afghan rebels) | 6 | 4.9 | 7 | 6.0 |
| UN action | 5 | 4.1 | 5 | 4.3 |
| Other world response | 2 | 1.6 | 4 | 3.4 |
| Allied response | 1 | .8 | 1 | .9 |
| Other | 6 | 4.9 | 4 | 3.4 |
| TOTAL FOREIGN | 68 | (55.3) | 65 | (55.9) |
| **Domestic Response** | | | | |
| US response and actions | 38 | 30.9 | 35 | 30.2 |
| Campaign | 7 | 5.7 | 7 | 6.0 |
| Interest groups | 7 | 5.7 | 4 | 3.4 |
| US/China | 3 | 2.4 | 5 | 4.3 |
| TOTAL DOMESTIC | 55 | (44.7) | 51 | (43.9) |
| TOTAL | 123 | 100.0 | 116 | 99.8 |

the high level of interest group involvement—12 and 14 percent respectively on NBC and CBS. This provides a sharp contrast, which will be examined, with the minimal reliance on interest group sources in the Cold War crises of the early sixties.

## THE FOREIGN STORY

The large US official source usage was of particular significance in relation to the foreign story. Overall source figures testify to the importance of the Administration in providing interpretation throughout. Analysis of the first ten days of coverage establishes that Administration and anti-Soviet rebel sources were used exclusively in stories dealing first with the impending Soviet action and then with the event itself. On both networks, the Administration's view went totally unchallenged from December 21 (when the first stories based on State Department background briefings appeared) through December 28 (when because of the crisis the president canceled both a weekend at Camp David and television debates with Kennedy and then formally charged the Soviets with an "invasion" of Afghanistan). The story was one of Soviet aggression, similar to the invasion of Czechoslovakia, but this time it was more threatening because the Soviets had moved out of their Warsaw Pact sphere of influence into an autonomous buffer state, thus endangering the Persian Gulf, only a day's march away.

Until December 31, the only foreign views of the situation quoted on either network, with the exception of one CBS anti-Soviet reaction story from Iran, were those of the "Muslim rebels" who were fighting the Soviets of Afghanistan. CBS interviewed a rebel leader in New York immediately, and pictures of the white-garbed rebels became the focal point of many subsequent stories: rebels hoisting the green flag of Islam or buying weapons at arms bazaars. Refugees in Iran and Pakistan were shown vowing to form guerilla groups and return. Throughout, they were depicted in heroic terms, determined to fight despite superior Soviet military force. Their reasons for fighting were given as an Islamic crusade against godless Marxism and modernization and as traditional rebellion against centralized authority.

The Soviet position was that the rebels were fighting with substantial outside assistance, including CIA training and money from the Chinese, and that intervention was necessary to prevent the transformation of a friendly neighbor into a hostile state. This view was given no credence on either network. NBC stated at the outset that the rebels were receiving "no significant foreign support" (December 27, 1979) and ran no clarification of this view, even after it became clear on January 9 that the Chinese were giving to Pakistan millions of dollars in aid which was going to the rebels. The fact that this confirmed the Soviet viewpoint in at least one regard was not noted. Both networks broadcast pictorial stories showing the rebels buying homemade arms at Dharra bazaar in Pakistan. These stories had indicated that the rebels' other weapons were Soviet-made and either captured in battle or acquired through Afghan army defections. Despite the Chinese connection, these stories were allowed to stand.[1]

This picture was not greatly disturbed by the one hint of complexity in the issue of rebel motivation that came from a British freelance journalist, who had lived for a month with the rebels and therefore had rare firsthand experience. The journalist reported that money was a strong motivating factor and that the rebels were as interested in capturing Soviet weapons to sell for personal gain as in using them to build a movement to fight the Russians.[2]

The issue for journalists then became one of outwitting the Soviets, who had lied from the beginning on such questions as whether the pro-Soviet Afghan leader, Babrak Karmal, was in Kabul at the time of the coup. The majority of the Afghan rebel and Soviet response stories, which together comprised half of the foreign story segments, dealt with the size of the Soviet military presence and the military prospects of the rebels (see Table 7.2.) This was clearly the main focus for television journalists, who were confined first to the Kabul airport and then to their hotel during the two weeks between January 2 and 17. On the latter date they were ordered out of the country for "creating incidents." They had tried to photograph Soviet military installations and to determine the nature of the fighting taking place just beyond the high mountains which surround Kabul and from which all, including the television audience, could hear the tantalizing rumble of gunfire. Stories from Kabul focused on whatever Soviet tanks, trucks, or soldiers were locally visible. Shooting these pictures quickly brought them into conflict with the Soviets. The exiting Don Kladstrup of CBS noted on January 18 that "over the past two and a half weeks reporters from other countries have been shot at, detained, and threatened with jail terms for trying to take pictures of the Soviet military presence here." Reporters speculated on the basis of rebel, United States, and "Western" observers as to the sizes of the Soviet forces and of the rebel contingents combatting them.

The earliest stories magnified rebel successes. This was particularly true on NBC (December 27), where the "holy war" of the *mujajeddin* (freedom fighters) was described as having won the support of 50 percent of the

---

[1] Charges that the rebels were receiving CIA assistance were not explored despite a *New York Times* report on February 16 that "rumors that a CIA covert operation had begun to help supply Afghan insurgents starting circulating in Washington in the second week in January." The *New York Times* was similarly silent until July 21, 1980, when Drew Middleton examined discrepancies in official statements on the issue and cited various reasons for Administration secrecy.

[2] See the CBS story January 10, 1980. For a newspaper view see Middleton (1979). Middleton commented that the question was whether "the rebels will use their captured weapons against the Afghan Army and the Russians or against neighboring tribes."

population. Such statistics later proved to be as uncertain as the communications system in a country with deserts, high mountains, few roads, and Soviet roadblocks. It was impossible to know even whether battles reported by the half-dozen rebel groups headquartered in Peshawar, just across the Khyber Pass in Pakistan, had actually taken place—much less what part of the population was supporting whom. Print and television reporters alike were embarrassed by reporting battles which did not take place and by giving dubious accounts of Afghan army defections and Soviet army intentions: some acknowledged the problems due to information based on low standards of accuracy.

Accuracy was a problem in Washington where White House press spokesmen allowed guesses to pass as accurate statistics and gave the impression that Soviet forces were headquartered in Herat, on the historic route to Iran, and were perhaps poised to proceed on to the Persian Gulf (see Gwertzman, 1980). Accuracy was also a problem in Kabul, where an official in the American Embassy gave out wildly inflated information, and in Peshawar, where the rebels gave out information later seen as quite inaccurate. Like the greater part of the 187 western media representatives registered at the Intercontinental Hotel in Kabul during the second week in January, television reporters were largely "firemen" on the scene rather than journalists with long experience. Naturally, it took them a while to adjust to the local "tall tale" tradition which was affecting Western and non-Western sources alike (Auerbach, 1980); Steif, 1980). But the issue of reliability emerged later. During the critical weeks on television in late December and early January, the battle of the rebels against the Soviet Union was as starkly etched against the mountains facing north as was the image of the gun-toting Zbigniew Brzezinski.

If the rebel movement was viewed through the White House lens, so were other aspects of the foreign story. Only 0.8 percent of the story segments on both networks focused on the Allied reactions, and there were no stories from European capitals offering their interpretations of why the Soviets invaded Afghanistan. A paucity of European sources was quoted—an average of only one half of one percent of the sources on both networks. (The figure for the "unidentified Western diplomats and observers" category was somewhat higher, and this category presumably included some unidentified West European sources.) See Tables 7.2 and 7.3.

Europeans served primarily as stage props to highlight the actions of the president during this critical period of United States response. There were Dulles Airport stories depicting the president's emissary, Warren Christopher, setting off to Europe to gain support for the president's previously announced (January 4), hardline response to the Soviets. Such a story, on January 13, was concerned with what the emissary had to say: that he expected the Allies "not to undercut us, but to support us." There was no report on how the Allies themselves might feel about the American policies already announced.

Table 7.3
Sources Quoted*

| | NBC seconds | NBC percent | CBS seconds | CBS percent |
|---|---|---|---|---|
| White House** | 1130 | 26.4 | 932 | 16.3 |
| Agriculture Dept. | 200 | 4.7 | 139 | 2.4 |
| Commerce Dept. | 0 | 0 | 5 | .1 |
| Defense Dept. | 145 | 3.4 | 411 | 7.2 |
| State Dept. & Intelligence | 458 | 10.7 | 726 | 12.7 |
| TOTAL US OFFICIALS | 1933 | 45.1 | 2213 | 38.7 |
| Domestic Politicians | 114 | 2.7 | 379 | 6.6 |
| Interest Groups | 541 | 12.6 | 821 | 14.3 |
| Americans Living in Kabul | 35 | .8 | 0 | 0 |
| New York Police | 10 | .2 | 0 | 0 |
| Former US Govt. Officials | 0 | 0 | 94 | 1.6 |
| TOTAL US DOMESTIC (INC. US OFFICIALS) | 2633 | 61.4 | 3507 | 61.2 |
| USSR | 476 | 11.1 | 274 | 4.8 |
| Afghanistan Officials | 221 | 5.2 | 428 | 7.5 |
| Other Afghan | 241 | 5.6 | 345 | 6.0 |
| Middle East (Inc. Iran & Israel) | 239 | 5.6 | 377 | 6.6 |
| Pakistan | 16 | .4 | 273 | 4.8 |
| Europe | 33 | .8 | 21 | .4 |
| Latin America | 9 | .2 | 95 | 1.7 |
| Canada | 24 | .6 | 57 | 1.0 |
| India | 11 | .3 | 25 | .4 |
| Poland | 0 | 0 | 24 | .4 |
| China | 39 | .9 | 76 | 1.3 |
| Japan | 13 | .3 | 15 | .3 |
| Intnl. Olympic Committee | 33 | .8 | 0 | 0 |
| Amnesty International | 18 | .4 | 0 | 0 |
| Nonaligned Countries | 5 | .1 | 0 | 0 |
| Nonwestern Diplomats & Observers | 15 | .4 | 0 | 0 |
| Western Diplomats & Observers | 238 | 5.6 | 209 | 3.7 |
| Australia | 6 | .1 | 0 | 0 |
| Bangladesh | 14 | .3 | 0 | 0 |
| TOTAL FOREIGN | 1651 | 38.7 | 2219 | 38.9 |
| TOTAL | 4284 | 100.1 | 5726 | 100.1 |

* Table includes time given to direct on-air statements of sources, and to newscaster paraphrasing or direct quotation of sources.
** Includes Presidential quotes. See Table 7.7 for Presidential quotes alone.

Christopher's twenty seconds in this story were only one second short of the total time the Allies were quoted in any Afghan-related story on CBS. Nine of Europe's remaining twenty-one seconds on CBS were devoted to a network one liner immediately following the president's January 4 speech, a speech which was startling in its failure even to hint at what was destined to become a major issue in allied relations. After devoting one minute and thirty-four seconds to the president's speech and further United States plans to move against the Soviets, CBS (January 5) devoted nine seconds to the Allied reaction: "In general, Western governments applauded Mr. Carter's speech last night." Only the British were quoted, however, to the effect that Soviet Foreign Minister Gromyko was told to call off a visit to London.

A reporter interested in Western viewpoints might have sought other reactions as well. France and West Germany, for example, did not appreciate the president's taking matters into his own hands. By early February, the British Prime Minister was forced to retreat as a European position developed urging neutralization and noninterference by both Soviets and Americans.[3] Western Europeans believed that the Soviet Union should be condemned, but rejected the U.S. view that the Soviet Union was solely responsible for destabilizing the situation and that harsh economic sanctions should be applied. The French were not quoted at all on network television.

Similarly, short shrift was given to historical or economic arguments which might have supported the European reluctance to impose sanctions. The Soviet Union is still a major producer of crude oil, and Europe imports a large volume of Soviet oil each day. West Germany is particularly dependent on Soviet energy resources. Such facts were not mentioned despite the president's explanation that a major reason for the U.S. action was to protect the Western oil supply. Also unmentioned was that this new hardline American policy came after several years of encouraging Western Europe to develop trade with the Soviet Union. Instead, NBC's leading story (January 16) dealing with Europe's views concentrated on President Carter's gratification that the Soviets were "chastened and surprised" by the world's reaction to the boycott. John Chancellor continued with an unadorned and caustic comment: "They make sympathetic noises but evidently the West Europeans don't want to hurt their trade with the Soviets."

Western European nations, it is sometimes pointed out, receive more media coverage than other nations, in part because they are culturally similar and familiar allies. In this crisis situation, however, European views which ran counter to those of the United States government were not explored on network television.

---

[3] Airport stories occurred January 7 and 8 on both networks and January 13 on CBS. The one-liner was on CBS on January 5. For the evolving story of Europeans and the embargo, see Lewis (1980) and Downie (1980).

Quoted most extensively were leaders of Middle Eastern and south-west Asian countries. These leaders are listed in Table 7.4 and are characterized in terms of whether or not they were opposed to the Soviet action, and ranked by total amount of time given to their quoted or paraphrased views. President Sadat, a linchpin of US policy, received the greatest attention. At the outset of the crisis, he talked for nearly five minutes with Walter Cronkite and declared that the United States was already "at war with the USSR to control oil. . . it is the battle of Western civilization."

Second billing went to the drama surrounding the American courtship of Pakistan's President Zia ul-Haq, whose country assumed special strategic significance. President Zia ul-Haq was interviewed extensively concerning whether United States assistance to Pakistan should be increased. He termed Soviet charges that Pakistan was training and equipping Afghan rebels "slanders of sinister and mischievous design." He was also depicted in troop review ceremonies as a good political "campaigner' out among the tribes in

**Table 7.4**
**Sources: Middle East and Southwest Asian Countries**

|  | Seconds of News Time | |
|---|---|---|
|  | NBC | CBS |
| **Opposed to the Soviet Action** | | |
| Egypt | 41 | 290 |
| Pakistan | | |
|   Zia ul-Haq | 8 | 124 |
|   Unidentified | 8 | 31 |
|   F.M. Aga Shahi | | 10 |
|   UN Ambassador | | 19 |
|   Tribal leaders | | 8 |
|   Hospital Officials | | |
|   Peshawar | | 81 |
| TOTAL PAKISTAN | 16 | 273 |
| Iran | | |
|   General | 11 | |
|   Revolutionary Council | 10 | |
|   Students | 30 | |
|   Ghotzbadeh | 31 | 17 |
| TOTAL IRAN | 82 | 17 |
| Muslin Countries (collectively) | 50 | 7 |
| Israel | 13 | 27 |
| Oman | 30 | |
| Kuwait | | 20 |
| Bahrein | 17 | |
| United Arab Emirates | | 16 |
| Saudi Arabia | 7 | |
| **Not Opposed to Soviet Action** | | |
| Afghan Government of Babrak Karmal | 241 | 345 |
| India | 11 | 25 |

Western Pakistan, an area which was closely examined for softness as a possible new front for Soviet advances (CBS, December 31, January 13 and 18).

Quotes from Iran and from what were collectively termed the "Muslim countries" ranked third and fourth as Muslim opposition to a great power other than the United States became a newsworthy event. Finally, Israel received special notice as Prime Ministers Begin and Sadat met with the pyramids in the background and agreed on opposition to the Soviet Union. All other leaders quoted represented strategically important oil-producing countries. They were also asked whether modernization was affecting their stability.

The Palestine Liberation Organization was not quoted on the invasion. The only indication that the PLO had a position was NBC's comment that the Egyptian delegate walked out during the debate on the issue at the United Nations when the PLO representative presented his views. The greater story was in what John Chancellor termed (January 14) the fact that "never before had so many nonaligned and Muslim nations lined up against the Soviet Union—and, indeed, it was newsworthy that the Soviet action was overwhelmingly condemned in the General Assembly, which called for troop withdrawal.

Overall quoting patterns thus reflected the issue as defined in American terms. Only two governments in Asia, India and the Afghan government of Babrak Karmal, were quoted as opposing United States policies.

## REPORTER INFERENCE

In order to determine not only who was quoted but how they were quoted, all commentators were ranked for inference, whether positive or negative in either pre- or post-quotation remarks about a source. Story segments which did not contain such inference were termed neutral. Positive inference was defined as verbal usage or tonal inflection that implied justification or acceptance of a source or its views. Negative inference was the reverse and involved verbal and tonal usage that discounted the views of a source. Overall such inferences were infrequent. This finding confirms the view that television newscasters are themselves generally neutral; it suggests that the distortion which is sometimes ascribed to television coverage of foreign affairs derives more from source selection patterns.

Instances of evaluative reporter inferences did occur, however, and in similar measures on both networks: in 17 story segments or 14.6 percent of the total on CBS, and in 14 segments or a total of 11.3 percent of all story segments on NBC. It also occurred more frequently in relation to foreign governments, with all of the instances on NBC and two-thirds of those on CBS directed against foreign sources. The implication is that a different standard of reporter commentary does apply with regard to foreign governments that expressed views opposed to those of the United States. The Soviet Union was more frequently quoted in a negative way, with the highest level of reporter inference occurring in relation to the Soviets and the "puppet" government of Babrak Karmal (see Table 7.5).

Negative inferences on CBS, for example, took the form of stressing the untrustworthiness of the Soviet Union by pointing out the discrepancies between earlier and later Soviet statements (December 27, 1979). It also took the form of word usage which indicated that a lack of credence should be given to Soviet interpretations of United States actions. Soviet actions pointing to the crimes of previous regimes were considered devious attempts to divert attention from the current Soviet invasion (January 14, 1980).

Criticism on NBC took the form of verbal usage which probably would not have been applied to a Western government. The Soviets were said to make a "strident attack" on President Carter (January 22, 1980), not a "strong" attack. Similarly, the Soviets alone launched a "propaganda" campaign (January 10, 1980).

The few times that Argentina and India (two countries not following the United States lead) were quoted, the negativity expressed in relation to these sources was significant. Argentina's pretensions to independent political judgment were deflated by Cronkite's comment when they failed to respond to an American plea to halt grain shipments: "That presumably means they'll fill Soviet orders if the price is right" (January 14).

While there were few positive inferences for the positions of most foreign governments on the Afghan issue, China was an exception. Beginning January 5 several lead stories came from network reporters who followed Defense Secretary Harold Brown to China. Brown and the Chinese leaders received ceremonial coverage touring naval yards and guided missile facilities and toasting the coordination of defense efforts along what Brown termed separate but parallel tracks. Commentators on both networks remarked that China was a defensive country in contrast to the Soviet Union.

Walter Cronkite set the tone for China coverage, remarking in a lead story that "the Soviet occupation of Afghanistan is a direct threat to China, which has few friendly countries along its borders" (January 9). Similarly, an NBC newscaster said (January 12) that the Chinese were interested only in increasing their defensive might through cooperation with the United States and would not use military force to "influence the balance of power" as the United States and the Soviet Union do. That China had already sent tens of millions of dollars worth of arms to Pakistan "much of which has already been sent to rebels fighting in Afghanistan" (CBS, January 9) was not discussed in terms of the balance of power. America's clearly expressed hope to turn China into a modern military power—part of a historic rapprochement for the United States, China, and Japan—was not mentioned

## Table 7.5
## Anchor-Reporter Inferences Toward Sources

| | Negative | | | | Positive | | | |
|---|---|---|---|---|---|---|---|---|
| | CBS (N = 12) | % | NBC (N = 14) | % | CBS (N = 5) | % | NBC (N = 1) | % |
| **Foreign Sources** | | | | | | | | |
| USSR | 5 | 41.7 | 8 | 57.1 | | | | |
| Karmal Government (Soviet-backed) | 1 | 8.3 | 5 | 35.7 | | | | |
| Khomeini | | | 1 | 7.1 | | | | |
| Indira Gandhi | 1 | 8.3 | | | | | | |
| Argentina | 1 | 8.3 | | | | | | |
| Afghan Rebels & Refugees | | | | | 1 | 20.0 | | |
| China | | | | | 2 | 40.0 | 1 | 100. |
| UN | | | | | 1 | 20.0 | | |
| **Domestic Sources** | | | | | | | | |
| Carter Administration | 2 | 16.7 | | | 1 | 20.0 | | |
| Kennedy "people" | 1 | 8.3 | | | | | | |
| Bush "people" | 1 | 8.3 | | | | | | |
| TOTAL | 12 | 99.9 | 14 | 99.9 | 5 | 100.0% | 1 | 100. |

117

on either network as a possible impetus for a new sense of Soviet isolation underlying the invasion of Afghanistan. Amid the coverage of Chinese motivation as seen through the prism of Defense Secretary Brown, there was no comparable examination of Soviet motivations.

## PROTECTING THE PRESIDENT IN STORIES FOREIGN AND DOMESTIC

Network television dealt with the primary antagonist of the United States in an additional way. Television news stacked their sources against the Soviets and in favor of the president. Furthermore, the president was set above the raucous clamor of domestic debate on the subject and was juxtaposed instead to the Soviets.

To examine what sort of balance occurs on a foreign story such as the Afghan one, the source context was examined for stories involving quotes by the Russians, President Carter, Agriculture Secretary Bergland, Senator Edward Kennedy[4] and the International Longshoremen's Association (ILA). All of those who supported, were neutral, or opposed the position of these protagonists were tallied. What emerged was an interesting double standard.

The views of Agriculture Secretary Bergland and Senator Kennedy were balanced against each other and against other domestic sources— particularly among the economic and Moscow Olympics interest groups affected by the president's boycott policies, whose views accounted for a substantial percentage of sources quoted on the Afghan issue (see Tables 7.3 and 7.6). A different standard was applied to the views of the president and the Soviets.

The Soviets were never quoted alone. Quotation of the Soviets always occurred in the context of other sources which usually discredited them. Averaging the two networks together, the Soviets were quoted in the context of opposing quotations 72 percent of the time (Table 7.7).

The opposite occurred in the case of President Carter, who was quoted in a decidedly supportive context. This held true for both networks, although there was more pronounced presidential support on NBC than on CBS. In a quoting pattern almost exactly opposite that of the Soviets, the president was depicted with supporting sources an average of 76.5 percent of the time (73.4 on CBS and 79.8 on NBC.) Most of these supporting sources were domestic. In the case of CBS, 60.8 percent, and NBC, 100 percent, came from within the Administration.

---

[4] All segments were included which were relevant to the issue which was raised in either the Soviet, the Presidential, or the Kennedy quote. These quotes might be in the middle of the story or elsewhere. In the case of the Soviet Union, a number of quotes in all segments of a particular day's Afghan stories were included, because all these dealt with the issue of Soviet behavior and international reaction. The exceptions were Olympic and economic boycott stories which were purely issues of domestic debate.

**Table 7.6**
**Interest Group Coverage***

| | (Seconds) NBC | % Total | (Seconds) CBS | % Total |
|---|---|---|---|---|
| **Embargo Issue** | | | | |
| Farm Bureau | 25 | 4.6 | | |
| Natl. Farmers Org. | | | 15 | 1.8 |
| "Farmers" | 28 | 5.2 | 121 | 14.7 |
| Grain Analysts | 52 | 9.6 | 22 | 2.7 |
| Board of Trade | 25 | 4.6 | 17 | 2.1 |
| Traders in Chicago | | | 60 | 7.3 |
| Amer. Agricultural Movement | | | 138 | 16.8 |
| Intnl. Longshoremen's Assn. | 89 | 16.5 | 75 | 9.1 |
| West Coast Longshoremen | 6 | 1.1 | | |
| AFL-CIO | 10 | 1.8 | | |
| Transportation Workers | 5 | .9 | | |
| Teamsters | 11 | 2.0 | | |
| Occidental Petroleum | | | 10 | 1.2 |
| "Patriotic Scuba Divers" | | | 12 | 1.5 |
| SUBTOTAL | 251 | 46.3 | 470 | 57.2 |
| **Olympic Boycott** | | | | |
| US Olympic Committee | 50 | 9.2 | 65 | 7.9 |
| Olympic Athletes | 208 | 38.4 | 160 | 19.5 |
| SUBTOTAL | 258 | 47.6 | 160 | 19.5 |
| **Other** | | | | |
| Vietnam Veterans | | | 101 | 12.3 |
| African-American Inst. | | | 12 | 1.5 |
| Newspapers & Magazines | 32 | 5.9 | 78 | 9.5 |
| SUBTOTAL | 32 | 5.9 | 191 | 23.3 |
| TOTAL | 541 | 99.8 | 821 | 100.0 |

* (12.6 percent of total news source time)

Averaging the two networks together, the president was set up against opposing sources only 19.7 percent of the time, and most of these, 73.9 percent, were foreign sources. CBS, however, set the president against domestic opponents twice as often as did NBC. Thirty-six percent of the opposing sources were domestic on CBS, compared to 16 percent on NBC. NBC more frequently put the president against foreign sources, notably the Soviets and the Afghans, who, as noted earlier, were discredited in other ways on network television. These two governments were the president's primary antagonists; 93.2 percent of the president's opposing sources on NBC, and 67.3 percent on CBS, were the Soviet or Afghan governments.

CBS was somewhat more likely to present credible foreign critics next to segments quoting the president. These critics, however, turned out not to be terribly formidable. Lord Killanin, president of the International Olympic Committee, was given five seconds against the president and the Agriculture Secretary on the issue of whether the Olympics should be moved out

Table 7.7
Context of Quotations of President Carter and the Soviet Union

| | President Carter | | | | Soviet Union | | | |
|---|---|---|---|---|---|---|---|---|
| | CBS* | % | NBC* | % | CBS* | % | NBC* | % |
| Principal | 280 | 46.6 | 765 | 53.6 | 230 | 21.0 | 400 | 30.5 |
| Supporting Sources | 220 | 26.9 | 372 | 26.1 | 27 | 2.5 | 8 | 0.6 |
| Opposing Sources | 171 | 20.9 | 262 | 18.4 | 839 | 76.5 | 902 | 68.9 |
| Neutral Sources | 46 | 5.6 | 27 | 1.9 | 0 | 0.0 | 0 | 0.0 |
| TOTAL TIME | 817 | 100.0 | 1426 | 100.0 | 1096 | 100.0 | 1310 | 100.0 |
| Supporting Sources: | | | | | | | | |
|   US Government | 118 | 53.7 | 292 | 78.5 | 0 | 0.0 | 0 | 0.0 |
|   US Non-government | 76 | 34.5 | 0 | 0.0 | 0 | 0.0 | 0 | 0.0 |
|   Foreign | 26 | 11.8 | 80 | 21.5 | 27 | 100.0 | 8 | 100.0 |
| TOTAL TIME | 220 | 100.0 | 372 | 100.0 | 27 | 100.0 | 8 | 100.0 |
| Opposing Sources: | | | | | | | | |
|   US Domestic | 61 | 35.7 | 43 | 16.4 | 390 | 46.5 | 690 | 76.5 |
|   USSR/Afghan govt. | 74 | 43.2 | 204 | 77.9 | 0 | 0.0 | 0 | 0.0 |
|   Other Foreign | 36 | 21.1 | 15 | 5.7 | 449 | 53.5 | 212 | 23.5 |
| TOTAL TIME | 171 | 100.0 | 262 | 100.0 | 839 | 100.0 | 902 | 100.0 |
| Principal quoted alone | 10 | 1.2 | 258 | 18.1 | 0 | 0.0 | 0 | 0.0 |
| Principal quoted in context of other sources | 807 | 98.8 | 1168 | 81.9 | 1096 | 100.0 | 1310 | 100.0 |

* time in seconds

of Moscow. Unidentified Pakistani military leaders gave their view that it was the fault of the United States that they were confronting the Soviet Union with "museum pieces."

Overall, CBS gave the president considerably less coverage than did NBC (see Table 7.7). NBC, for example, on the day before the Iowa precinct caucuses included a John Chancellor interview with Mr. Carter and lengthy crisis segments from *Meet the Press*.

Intra-Administration divisions may prompt articles in newspapers which reflect both sides and which report the debate.[5] The complexities which haunted the State Department did appear in newspaper articles at this time (Osnos, 1979), but television was little affected by this.

Differences between the White House and the State Department were referred to only once and in a simplified fashion. The story considered whether differences between the White House and the State Department might conceivably lead to war by creating the illusion of US weakness. Secretary Vance's reluctance to threaten nuclear war if the Soviets invaded Iran through Afghanistan was singled out as the root of the difficulty.

---

[5] See Montague Kern (1979) for a discussion of the effect of intra-Administration debate on the foreign policy coverage of Washington-oriented newspapers.

While there were no subtle interpretations of intra-Administration differences, CBS did briefly raise the issue of Administration competence. In the one and only case of an opposing quotation from within the Administration's ranks, the former Ambassador to Iran, Malcom Toon, was shown expressing his astonishment that Carter was surprised at the Soviet invasion of Afghanistan since he had warned Carter of this possibility "almost every day."

With the exception of these instances of slightly more critical coverage on CBS, the president was allowed to define the issues. Only once was the president confronted with the criticism of politicians. In a story a few days before the Iowa GOP debate, Republican candidates were shown criticizing Carter for weakness and inquiring what incredible mistakes had caused the Soviets to think they could get away with such a challenge. Two days later the president outlined his response to the Soviets—economic sanctions and military buildup. Republicans who opposed the economic sanctions during the debates were not heard from thereafter, except very briefly on January 21;[6] meanwhile, the president wore the mantle of patriotism.

President Carter was also quoted only once on each network in the same story with Senator Kennedy, his other critic on foreign policy issues, who similarly challenged the president on the embargo issue. Kennedy's coverage illustrates one aspect of the difficulties a challenger faces in confronting an incumbent president. Carter's comments were news stories defining the nature of a foreign threat and the American response. By contrast, Kennedy's views were depicted, in all of the nine stories in which they appeared, in terms of whether they would help or hurt him in the campaign. Overall, on the two networks, Kennedy was equally balanced with opposing views (Table 7.8).

While the president was rarely quoted in the context of politicians and was never depicted as dealing with the issue in a political fashion, the opposite was true for Kennedy. Also, unlike Carter, Kennedy was quoted with no supporting sources. In one NBC story, for example, Kennedy was shown responding to a charge by Vice President Mondale, a charge that was never balanced or neutralized by any views other than Kennedy's own. Mondale quite starkly challenged Kennedy's patriotism. Kennedy replied by questioning how Vice President Mondale could doubt his patriotism or that of any member of his family. The challenge remained, however, and the embargo (for which one might also read patriotism) was later described on CBS as the greatest issue dividing Kennedy and the President.[7]

---

[6] Republican quotes appeared on CBS on January 2, 3 and 21, and on NBC on January 3 and 21, 1980. The Republican views on the embargo issue were not quoted on network television.

---

[7] See stories on NBC, January 8, 10, 11, and 18; and on CBS, December 28, 1979, January 9, 10, 17, and 21, 1980.

**Table 7.8**
**Context of Quotations of Agriculture Secretary Bergland**
**Senator Edward Kennedy, and the International Longshoreman's Association**

| | Secretary Bergland | | | | Senator Kennedy | | | | Longshoremen (ILA) | | | |
|---|---|---|---|---|---|---|---|---|---|---|---|---|
| | CBS* | % | NBC* | % | CBS* | % | NBC* | % | CBS* | % | NBC* | % |
| Principal | 125 | 28.2 | 200 | 47.6 | 149 | 38.7 | 80 | 58.4 | 75 | 43.1 | 89 | 47.1 |
| Supporting Sources | 73 | 16.5 | 85 | 20.2 | 0 | 0.0 | 0 | 0.0 | 10 | 5.7 | 12 | 6.3 |
| Opposing Sources | 228 | 51.5 | 110 | 26.2 | 236 | 61.3 | 57 | 41.6 | 89 | 51.2 | 88 | 46.6 |
| Neutral Sources | 17 | 3.8 | 25 | 6.0 | 0 | 0.0 | 0 | 0.0 | 0 | 0.0 | 0 | 0.0 |
| TOTAL TIME | 443 | 100.0 | 420 | 100.0 | 385 | 100.0 | 137 | 100.0 | 174 | 100.0 | 189 | 100.0 |
| Supporting Sources: | | | | | | | | | | | | |
| US Government | 5 | 6.8 | 76 | 89.4 | 0 | | 0 | | 0 | 0.0 | 0 | 0.0 |
| US Non-govt. | 68 | 93.2 | 5 | 5.9 | 0 | | 0 | | 10 | 100.0 | 12 | 100.0 |
| Foreign | 0 | 0.0 | 4 | 4.7 | 0 | | 0 | | 0 | 0.0 | 0 | 0.0 |
| TOTAL TIME | 73 | 100.0 | 85 | 100.0 | 0 | | 0 | | 10 | 100.0 | 12 | 100.0 |
| Opposing Sources: | | | | | | | | | | | | |
| US Domestic | 223 | 97.8 | 100 | 90.9 | 236 | 100.0 | 57 | 100.0 | 89 | 100.0 | 88 | 100.0 |
| USSR/Afghan govt. | 0 | 0.0 | 0 | 0.0 | 0 | 0.0 | 0 | 0.0 | 0 | 0.0 | 0 | 0.0 |
| Other Foreign | 5 | 2.2 | 10 | 9.1 | 0 | 0.0 | 0 | 0.0 | 0 | 0.0 | 0 | 0.0 |
| TOTAL TIME | 228 | 100.0 | 110 | 100.0 | 236 | 100.0 | 57 | 100.0 | 89 | 100.0 | 88 | 100.0 |
| Principal quoted alone | 23 | 5.2 | 0 | 0.0 | 27 | 7.0 | 44 | 32.1 | 15 | 8.6 | 0 | 0.0 |
| Principal quoted in the context of other sources | 420 | 94.8 | 420 | 100.0 | 358 | 93.0 | 93 | 67.9 | 159 | 91.4 | 189 | 100.0 |

* time in seconds

Unlike the president, Kennedy was also pitted in three-fourths of the cases on both networks against politicians and campaign aides.[8] Under such circumstances, Kennedy had little opportunity to appear statesmanlike because a different standard of reporting was applied to this domestic dimension of the Afghan story.

It was not only Kennedy, however, who was taking the heat on domestic aspects of the story. If the president was above the domestic fray and was dealing with foreign governments, Agriculture Secretary Bergland was out in front deflecting domestic criticism. Analysis of the context within which Bergland was quoted indicates that he was subject to a context of quotation quite different from that of the president. Balance was much more clearly the goal, as it was in the case of Senator Kennedy. Bergland was pitted against farmers who were furious at the boycott and fearful of losing future sales of wheat and against grain dealers in Chicago who believed the Administration's policies would have a devastating effect on farm prices.

Bergland was not quoted as frequently with supporting sources as was the president, although considerably more frequently than was Kennedy: 44.7 percent of the time on CBS, and 67.9 percent of the time on NBC. The Agriculture Secretary was more frequently quoted with opposing quotes (38 percent as compared to the president's 19.7 percent) but less frequently than Kennedy's 51.4 percent (Tables 7.7 and 7.8). Thus the handling of the Agriculture Secretary confirms the different reporting standards for balancing controversial domestic views on Afghanistan.

Another aspect of the story, the revolt of the dockworkers, suggests the effectiveness of a domestic challenge to the Administration when that challenge is assisted by favorable television coverage. On the evening news, while Jody Powell was promising a substantive response to the Soviets in the president's pending speech, the East and Gulf Coast International Longshoremen's Association proposed a boycott of Soviet shipping. A five-minute story the next day dealt with the president's own boycott proposals announced in his speech the evening before along with the negative response of the farmers, who were quoted as thinking primarily about their pocketbooks. The dockers, whose motivation was said to be patriotism, were played against them in almost equal measure. The dockers intended to go beyond the president's position and did so. They blocked the loading of an additional eight million metric tons of grain promised the Soviets above the amount proposed by the Administration. The networks noted that such actions raised questions about the reliability of the United States as a trading partner, hurting Allied shipping interests and costing taxpayers

---

[8] On CBS, Kennedy was quoted three times against Mondale, once against Bergland, and once against Carter. On NBC, he was quoted once against Carter, twice against White House aides, and once against Mondale.

millions of dollars, although no one disputed the healthy patriotism of the dockers.

As in the case of Kennedy, the dockers were equally balanced with opposing sources (Table 7.8). Unlike him they were sometimes quoted with domestic supporters.[9] On CBS the dockworkers' primary antagonists were the hapless farmers, while on NBC they were pitted against the White House which was quoted as "reacting cautiously, and not wanting to be 'considered weak.'"[10] Visuals of several different ships and ports and the drama of multifaceted confrontation dominated the substantial twelve minutes and fifty seconds devoted to embargo stories containing docker segments. The dockers made their case on network television, thereby putting pressure on the president.

Whatever the exact impact of this coverage on the White House, at the time of the Iowa precinct caucuses the president announced a decision to buy up the additional grain which the dockworkers were blocking and which was threatening to clog the ports. The coverage was balanced, as in the case of Kennedy, but television coverage painted the East and Gulf Coast dockers, and the president who subsequently adopted their position, red, white, and blue.

## CONCLUSION

Television coverage of the Afghan crisis points to the two dimensional nature of foreign affairs reporting: different standards apply when foreign and domestic aspects of international affairs stories are covered. Source analysis also shows that the entire crisis story is given a strong domestic component.

The foreign story is viewed through a domestic prism. In the absence of domestic interests with clout sufficient to challenge the president, his views dominate. Complex issues are not explored and the matter is set in a confrontational framework. In a conflict between the United States and a major antagonist, various devices are used to bolster the leadership of the

---

[9] On January 9, John Chancellor concluded a story with a quote by an AFL-CIO spokesman that the dockworkers' strike was a "legitimate, responsible and proper demonstration of the patriotism of union members." Similarly, they received the support of the "patriotic scuba divers" in a story about their planting an explosive in a channel grain cargo ships might traverse. The International Longshoremen's and Warehousemen's Union, which did not close down the ports on the west coast, received six seconds and no chance to explain their opposing position.

---

[10] The farmers were the dockers' primary opponents on CBS, with 56 seconds of source time as compared to the dockers' only other opponent, the Agriculture Department, which was quoted for 33 seconds. The farmers were, as noted previously, not quoted in a manner which defined them as patriotic. The White House was the primary opponent on NBC, with 55 seconds as compared to 38 for the State Department, which was briefly quoted to the effect that unions should not make foreign policy.

president. These practices include presenting him primarily in opposition, not to domestic critics, but to his foreign opponents, and using sources strongly in his favor. This gives the president a tremendous advantage in the political process.

Conversely, the source decks are weighted against foreign opponents, who also suffer in the majority of news stories in which newscaster inference occurs. Views of US allies are largely ignored. It is also possible that standards of accuracy may not be upheld in crisis situations involving serious problems of access and a highly charged emotional atmosphere.

A presidential slant definitely exists in foreign affairs coverage. Unlike the views of domestic politicians, the president is quoted according to standards which appear to apply more to foreign than to domestic news and which make little attempt to carefully balance views. In the case of Afghanistan, this happened less on CBS than on NBC. The close analysis of sources during this period detected a difference between NBC and CBS coverage of the president, with the latter giving him less coverage and including sources which raised the issue of competence.

Many explanations have been offered to account for the nature of international affairs reporting. Both problems of access and the Administration's great advantage in controlling the release of information play their role. So does commercialism, which knows that the popular market prefers stories of simple conflict and familiar values. What James Reston called the "Afghanistanism" of the *New York Times,* with its stories about remote parts of the world even in quiet times, are clearly not marketable on the commercial networks.

There is also the question of intent.[11] Journalists aware of strong feelings of national consciousness during the Afghan invasion selected stories and sources deemed significant by domestic standards, which include, of course, patriotism. Commercialism is important, but so also may be a culturally based nationalism.[12] It has often been noted that the special responsibility of the foreign correspondent is to report events as they are seen from abroad. Television news clearly does not attempt to convey a

[11] Many scholars have tended to discount the role of values as a factor explaining the nature of television foreign affairs coverage. See for example, Doris Graber (1980, Chapters 3 and 9). This is due to the unsubstantiated nature of a great deal of the literature dealing with ideological bias. This study suggests that it may be worth giving further thought to the issue of values since this may be more of a problem in foreign than in domestic reporting; domestic news is watched by interests which can be antagonistic if they are not treated fairly.

[12] Cultural nationalism in foreign affairs coverage may occur, particularly in relation to an area such as the Middle East and Southwest Asia because the culture is so alien to Americans and journalists have little acquaintance with the history or language. The issue may be particularly acute for television reporters, who are more often "firemen" than experienced foreign correspondents. The issue is receiving serious consideration in the journalistic community in the wake of the Iranian experience. Consideration of this as an issue certainly takes nothing away from commercialism as a deservedly popular explanatory variable.

foreign perspective, but rather responds to the US outlook. What we saw in television coverage of the Afghan crisis is what we were: a nation fearful of American setbacks in the Middle East, and worried that the Soviet Union would take advantage of that weakness.

Another conclusion of this study is that there is a greater attempt to balance the domestic aspects of foreign affairs coverage. This applies to politicians, interest groups, and Administration representatives taking the heat for the president. Some of this domestic reporting about an emotional international issue may center on the issue of patriotism or its absence. For example, Vice President Mondale's questioning of Kennedy's patriotism went unchallenged by reporters or opposing sources, while the dockers' patriotism was confirmed by the networks, assisting their successful challenge of White House Policy.

Network television seems unlikely to allow a foreign government—especially one that lacks a constituency in the US—effectively to challenge the president during times of crisis. The only direct challenge permitted is that from a strong domestic constituency. A domestic interest group may be able to make its case on national television, even during a crisis, when all other signs point to great presidential powers of definition. Coverage of Afghanistan reflected many aspects of these double standards between domestic and foreign reporting of an international news story.

# REFERENCES

Auerbach, Stuart. 1980. Afghans' Hearsay War Often Deceives the Press. *Washington Post*, August 24, 1980, p. 21.

Downie, Leonard, Jr. 1980. Europeans Plan Own Afghan Strategy. *Washington Post*, February 16, 1980, p. 14.

Graber, Doris. 1980. *Mass Media and American Politics*. Washington, D.C.: Congressional Quarterly Press.

Gwertzman, Bernard. 1980. US Accuracy Code Relaxed Over Kabul. *New York Times*, January 26, 1980, p. 6.

Hofstetter, C. Richard. 1976. *Bias in the News: Network Television Coverage of the 1972 Election Campaign*. Columbus, Ohio: Ohio State University Press.

Kern, Montague. 1979. The Presidency and the Press: John F. Kennedy's Foreign Policy Crisis and the Politics of Newspaper Coverage. Ph.D. dissertation, Johns Hopkins University, Baltimore, Maryland.

Lewis, Paul. 1980. Common Market Proposes a Neutral Afghanistan with International Guarantees if Soviet Withdraws. *New York Times*, February 10, 1980, p. A8.

Middleton, Drew. 1980. Aides Disagree on Level of U.S. Arms Aid to Afghans. *New York Times*, July 21, 1980.

————·1980. New Soviet Motives Emerge. *New York Times*, January 1, 1980, p. 1.

Osnos, Peter. 1979. Detente is Dead, Arms Race Resumes. *Washington Post*, December 30, 1979, p. 1.

Robinson, Michael J. and Keven R. Appel. 1979. Network News Coverage of Congress. *Political Science Quarterly* 94 (Fall 1979): 407–18.

Steif, William. 1980. At the Front in Afghanistan. *The Progressive*, April, 1980, pp. 16–21.

# 8

# IRAN VS. US TV NEWS:
# THE HOSTAGE STORY OUT OF CONTEXT

## DAVID ALTHEIDE

Americans became interested in Iran during the fall of the Shah's government in late 1978. That interest was sustained by the subsequent rise and fall of two transitional leaders and by the Iranian revolution in 1979 which culminated when the Ayatollah Khomeini returned from exile and assumed control of the religious and secular affairs of the embattled country. However, Americans never entirely realized the seriousness of the situation in Iran or the stake and role of the United States in this faraway land until November 4, 1979. On that day the American embassy was occupied by dozens of Iranian "students"—later referred to as terrorists, militants, or kidnappers—who detained Americans as hostages. This chapter examines how television network news coverage portrayed the hostages, their captors, leadership in both the United States and Iran, and related issues.

## METHODS AND PERSPECTIVE

Data were obtained through content analysis of selected early evening newscasts for the three major networks, from November 4, 1979 through June 7, 1980.[1] When possible, identical dates for the three networks were included in the sample of programs studied. In order to explore trends in reporting, it was decided to examine each network report pertaining to

[1] Support for this study was provided by a research fellowship from the Television and Politics Study Program of the School of Public and International Affairs at George Washington University. The professional assistance from the staff of the Vanderbilt Television News Archive is also acknowledged.

Iran presented on several consecutive newscasts over the six-month period (Lichty, 1978, p. 115). Clusters of no less than five consecutive days were selected for this analysis; each month received nearly equal analysis. Periods of somewhat varying length were included, e.g., nine days in November; five days in February because the extent of coverage varied. The specific dates selected for news analysis in the present report are listed in Table 8.1 for each network.

Relevant news reports for the selected days and weeks were identified using Vanderbilt University's *Television News Index and Abstracts.* Following several days of viewing portions of the videotapes loaned from the Vanderbilt Archive, a two page protocol was constructed to facilitate systematic data collection.[2] Variables that were coded for each story included length of report; length of subreports; format; presenter; origin of report; sources, names, and status of individuals interviewed; their dress, appearance, and facility with English; what was filmed, and the correspondence between the audio and the visual images.

Additional sources of televised data were selected including ABC *Special Reports* and *Nightline* reports focusing mainly on Iran. These were reviewed because ABC provided the most special report coverage during this period, and began regular late night newscasts to provide routine in depth coverage of the Iranian situation.

The findings presented in this study are based on data from 375 news stories totaling some 664 minutes, or slightly more than 11 hours, plus approximately 10 hours of key *Special Reports* from ABC. A list of the early evening newscasts that were analyzed during each period under study is presented in Table 8.1.

In addition to recording these systematic data, the observer's interpretations of trends in reporting, notes of obvious omissions, errors of fact, and general impressions were typed following the completion of each protocol. These notes contributed to the subsequent coding and analysis of the data.

Other reports were also analyzed, including newspaper articles, news magazine reports, some *MacNeil/Lehrer Reports*, and typed transcripts of some network stories prior to November 4, 1979, pertaining to the situation in Iran. These materials provided additional useful information for interpreting the data, and offered historical perspective.

---

[2] Several points should be made about the coding of these data. First, it was not always possible or desirable to maintain exclusive and exhaustive categories. Within a given news report, two or more topics may be mentioned by two or more parties. For this reason, total frequencies on various topics may exceed the total number of news reports analyzed. Second, both as a visual and aural medium, television can provide two or more bits of information relevant to this study within a period of a few seconds. For example, "hostage families," one topic in this study, included several subcategories, such as "at holidays" and "supportive of State Department." For presentational purposes, these have all been collapsed. In some instances a story may be coded as both "hostage family" and "private diplomacy," if that family was involved in individual efforts to free a hostage.

Table 8.1
Newscasts Analyzed (Nov. 1979–June 1980)

| Period | Month | ABC | CBS | NCB |
|--------|-------|-----|-----|-----|
| 1 | November 1979 | 4, 6–9, 11, 12 | 5–12 | 4–10, 12 |
| 2 | December 1979 | 24–28, 30, 31 | 24–28 | 24, 26–28 |
| 3 | January 1980 | 7–11 | 7–11 | 7–11 |
| 4 | February 1980 | 25–29 | 25–29 | 25–29 |
| 5 | March 1980 | 17–21 | 17–21 | 17–21 |
| 6 | April 1980 | 14–18 | 14–18 | 14–18 |
| 7 | May 1980 | 1, 2, 4–9 | 1–9 | 1, 2, 4–9 |
| 8 | June 1980 | 2–6 | 2–7 | 2–7 |

These data on network news coverage of the Iranian hostage situation offer an ideal basis for exploring a number of key questions about network news in particular and about the mass media in general. One question is how much the news media report reality or how much they define, select, and then report, in an acceptable format, those features of an event that are compatible with organizational considerations such as maintaining a lively, entertaining presentation. If the latter, as a plethora of research has demonstrated (Epstein, 1973; Batscha, 1975; Altheide, 1976; Altheide & Snow, 1979; Tuchman, 1978), then the nature of news coverage is inextricably bound to the reporting process itself.

A related question is the extent to which differing news emphases, over time, reflect the changing character of an event or reflect instead news values, including commercial considerations. To what extent are the people involved in news events, including reporters, selfconscious about the nature of newswork and news values in their activities and comments? To what extent does sustained news coverage of an episode provide additional detailed information and a deeper understanding for the audience? In what respect do the tools of TV news (specifically, the various film, visual, and transmitting technologies) contribute to the emphasis and omissions of reports? Finally, how do news personnel attempt to clarify their own role in the way events are reported, including the consequences of reporting about particular events over a period of time?

Such questions can be examined by studying the coverage of an event or series of events over a period of time. Comparing how three networks present reports (including the use of film, main analytic subjects, and overall style and mode of emphasis) provides a way to clarify further the nature of organizational processes which may characterize current news practices. Moreover, careful scrutiny of stories can illuminate reportorial strategies. Is the reporter's aim to understand and clearly present complexities, and even contradictions and ironies? Or, is the aim to get the hostages out, to castigate the obvious "enemies," and to lead the viewing audience into orgiastic support for certain positions? In short, what is the role and self-defined orientation of broadcast journalists covering international news? Their approach should be examined through actual news practices and news stories rather than through journalistic rhetoric of impartiality and truth seeking. Partial or complete answers to these questions will contribute to an understanding of the role of TV news in daily life and especially in international affairs.

## IRAN ON THE NEWS AGENDA

All three networks presented numerous reports about the hostage situation in Iran. The totals in Table 8.2 cover a period of approximately 50 days for each network from November 4, 1979, through June 7, 1980. Several points are apparent from this table. First, the networks were fairly similar in the number and length of time of their Iran stories. NBC, for the days selected in this study, did present fewer reports, and therefore, less total time; this difference is partially accounted for by reporting discrepancies in periods two and seven.

Table 8.2 also shows a trend over time to present shorter reports, ranging from an average length of 2:07 during period one and 2:10 for period two, to slightly more than 1:00 for periods six, seven, and eight. The three network average tended to show a general decline in frequency and time of news reports about Iran following the first two observational periods.

These trends in number of reports and time per report reflect several aspects of news coverage of the Iranian situation. The novelty rapidly diminished. News coverage that resulted from initial reactions and comments on reactions from officials, families, allies, and international organizations had already occurred. Even during the initial two-month period, there was considerable repetition. Still another consideration is that each of the networks began carrying "special reports;" ABC began such reports on a nightly basis. Perhaps the central feature of this declining coverage, which by most standards was still quite extensive, was that the event of the hostage taking was "old news," and the immediate efforts to free the hostages were not successful. News of Iran later consisted of reports and speculation on "new developments," "breakthroughs," "signs of encouragement," the "status" and "health" of the former Shah, and any events which might have bearing on the hostages' future. These generally included pronouncements by international organizations such as the ruling by the International Court of Justice and the resolution by the United Nations as well as US efforts to use sanctions to exact Iranian cooperation and visits by clergy and others who actually "saw" the hostages.

Such intense coverage meant that CBS, for example, gave an average of about 11 minutes each night to Iran during the days examined in November, 1979. In May, 1980, CBS was still averaging 4 minutes 20 seconds each night. By television news norms, this represents extensive coverage. (For a full review of the status of the hostage story on the networks' agenda, see the introductory chapter by William Adams and Phillip Heyl.) The tenor of coverage was influenced by a variety of factors, not the least of which was its televised format.

## FORMATS, THEMES AND TOPICS

The role of formats in molding news reports can be seen through an examination of how the hostage story was presented. A format is a set of rules defining how news content is to be presented. Formats used by all three networks were quite similar in the use of time, in the emphasis on particular topics, and in the overall presentation. The typical format began with an anchorperson giving an overview of the report and then followed with one or more reporters adding a bit more information to what the anchorperson originally said, usually with a film or tape presentation. Finally, either the anchorperson or a reporter summarized what had been presented. Each story segment is ordinarily confined to no more than about two minutes, with rare exceptions. A network's report on the hostage situation may be made up of six or seven separate segments, totaling fourteen or fifteen minutes, while each individual report may last from one to two minutes.

This combination gives a unity to the overall presentation in which one major message (e.g., the American embassy was overrun) may be followed by a series of details along with reactions from various people and officials (e.g., congressional leaders, State Department and White House spokespersons, family members, other American citizens, some foreign leaders). For example, ABC's coverage on November 4, 1980, of the embassy takeover consisted of three reports, two of which lasted 1:20 and 1:30 and the third lasting ten seconds, the minimal amount essential to be counted in this study.

The first segment dealt with what happened in the embassy takeover. It was introduced and then summed up by reporter Sam Donaldson's comments regarding who was responsible for the seizure. Donaldson said, in referring to the Ayatollah Khomeini, "It does appear to have his blessings." There was then an immediate cut to a segment by Ted Koppel who reported on the State Department's groping for an understanding of what happened and what should be done. Koppel and Donaldson then discussed the degree of responsibility of Khomeini, and Donaldson added that this could lead to some kind of U.S. military action, something with which no officials had been publicly associated. The anchorperson then briefly noted that some Iranian students had chained themselves to the Statue of Liberty as a demonstration against the Shah, who was being treated in New York for cancer.

The brevity of the initial reports can be explained in terms of general paucity of resources, both spoken and film, upon which to draw. Within two days, however, as reporters were dispatched to the key scenes, there emerged the major format for coverage which would persist until American journalists were expelled from Iran in the third week of January 1980.

One major consequence of the formatted news effort was to present a sense of rapidity of action on the part of the United States. The rapid fire electronic switching from one reporter to another—usually for taped reports—generated a dramatic sense of activity. For example, on November 6, 1979, ABC presented six reports lasting over ten minutes. The focus and scenes for these reports were, respectively:

1. Iranian protests against the United States (Tehran)
2. State Department spokesperson (State Department)
3. Report of resignation of Barzagan (State Department)
4. President Carter's domestic political problem with Iran (White House)
5. Hostage families (State Department's Iranian "situation room")
6. Protests against the Shah by Iranian students in the US (Philadelphia; Columbus, Ohio)

While the specifics would change (e.g., the student protests might be shown in Houston), the inclusion of statements, reactions, reactions to reactions, repeated themes, and new developments continued throughout the coverage. New events which would later occur, such as visits by clergy to the hostages, the deportation of Iranian students, and the rescue attempt, to name a few, would be inserted into the above format; in turn, they would be the "situation" to be explained, commented on, reacted to.

The format just described, while common to TV news reports and compatible with the effort to maintain a number of short, visual reports in order to keep the audience watching, did have a bearing on how the entire hostage situation was presented. This format was coupled with several major themes. First, the hostages were presented as victims, as innocent United States citizens, rather than as military personnel or foreign service personnel, who, by the very nature of their duties—all of which are still not clear at this writing—were serving the United States Government in a variety of ways. They were not, for the most part, defined as being in any kind of adversary relationship—actual or potential—to the government of

Iran, past, present, or still emerging. Indeed, virtually none of the less than obvious functions and duties of these individuals was ever discussed, other than that of being a "guard," a "specialist in Farsi," etc. They were "innocent" victims, not unlike any other American citizen in Iran, according to the news emphasis.

Related to this emphasis was news coverage of claims made by the Iranian militants to justify their actions in taking over the embassy. In the reports examined for this study, not one claim by the militants about espionage or conspiracy was ever acknowledged as a possibility by a journalist, nor were there any follow-up reports to further clarify what the activity of agency personnel had been. On November 9, ABC presented film from Iranian television regarding rooms and equipment within the embassy which were said to have been the location where plots against the Ayatollah Khomeini were hatched. When film of a bank of sophisticated electronic gear was shown, claimed by the militants to be espionage equipment, ABC's Bob Dyke described it as looking "like an expensive shortwave radio." In brief, the emphasis was on holding of the hostages, rather than any plausible foundation for their having been taken hostage in the first place. Iranians at the US embassy, as will be more evident further on, were systematically presented as being bellicose, irrational, and lacking any possible justification for their acts.

The thrust of some news reports was that all US citizens were in peril on the assumption that the United States of America was under attack in Iran. Complex as these claims may be, very little evidence was presented about the threat to non-embassy personnel. Indeed, many Americans were known to have remained in Iran during this time, although the networks offered very little discussion about them. One exception was a fifty-second interview with two American school teachers in Iran. When asked by ABC's Bob Dyke if they considered themselves brave, the reply was, "No, I consider myself a coward. There's nothing to be afraid of that we can see." They urged Americans not to base their opinion of the Iranian people on the actions of a few. These assertions were not followed up by any journalists during the periods covered by this study.

The main topics of coverage during the periods of this study show a rather consistent picture for all the networks (Table 8.3). In one sense this would be expected. Naturally, certain events would be highlighted, such as the rescue attempt in April which was continually covered throughout the first two weeks in May (period seven). News, after all, is presumably about timely events. In another sense, however, the nature of the focus over time cannot be explained solely by rather obvious events, but must be interpreted in the context of news formats as well as the peculiar advocacy themes adopted by the network reporters.

Network journalists came to define a variety of developments, such as the Iranian elections, from the vantage point of a single issue: getting the hostages released. It will be suggested that this orientation severely limited the nature and extent of topics presented. This approach, it will be further argued, tended to obfuscate important political, cultural, and religious aspects of the entire situation; in doing so it often confused rather than enlightened the audience.

Considerable emphasis was given to Iranian "external" and "internal" problems (Table 8.3). The former dealt mainly with Iran and the Soviet invasion of Afghanistan, skirmishes with Iraq, and sanctions from international organizations, and relations with some European countries. Coverage of "internal" problems focused on the various demonstrations, revolts, and other manifestations of dissatisfaction with the precepts of Ayatollah Khomeini, but more commonly, autocratic rule by Khomeini or the Shah. The longstanding feuds with the Kurds and with other ethnic groups in various provinces were seldom dealt with by the network news reports in any way other than showing dissatisfaction with Khomeini's rule.[3] (Demonstrations and gatherings of thousands of dissenters are, of course, visually interesting.)

The discussion that follows focuses on three topics that received much attention—the Shah of Iran, families of the hostages, and Iranian students in the United States—and on one topic that received little attention—religion in Iran. Use of sources and visual images will also be examined.

### THE SHAH

The Shah of Iran, as Table 8.3 indicates, was one of the most frequently covered of the subjects related to Iran. This total of 43 reports combines several dimensions of the Shah's coverage, including his status, health, wealth, liability, and history. Twenty-three of the reports on all three networks during these periods focused on his status, that is, which country was he in, where was he going, did he enjoy diplomatic immunity,

---

[3] On January 8, 1980, NBC's Ike Seamens, concluding a segment of "Iran Diary," told John Chancellor of the planned coverage of the next day's demonstrations in Tabriz: "That's right, John, we'll be in Tabriz where the demonstrations usually go against the Ayatollah Khomeini."

The next day's broadcast from Tabriz was censored, a move which led several reporters from several networks to complain about their privileges being increasingly restricted.

One exception to the largely superficial reports about internal dissent was a piece by NBC's Jim Bitterman in Zehedan, Baluchistan, aired December 24, 1979. His presentation of the complementary elements of extreme pluralism and anti-Khomeini sentiments was descriptively illustrated with film of Baluchistanis calmly walking and carrying weapons. In an unusual interview with a local leader, it was stressed that these people were more "pro-tribe" than anti-government. Bitterman also provided a review of the history of factionalism in this part of Iran.

## Table 8.2
### Number and Length of Stories about Iran During Each Period of Observation

| Period of Observation (see Table 8.1) | ABC | | | CBS | | | NBC | | | Period Avg. |
|---|---|---|---|---|---|---|---|---|---|---|
| | No. | Mins. | Net. Avg. | No. | Mins. | Net. Avg. | No. | Mins. | Net. Avg. | |
| 1 | 32 | 68 | (2:02) | 42 | 88 | (2:06) | 34 | 67 | (1:58) | (2:07) |
| 2 | 26* | 73* | (2:48) | 24 | 44 | (1:50) | 17 | 28 | (1:50) | (2:10) |
| 3 | 9 | 19 | (2:07) | 11 | 13 | (1:11) | 9 | 6 | (0:40) | (1:19) |
| 4 | 7 | 10 | (1:26) | 9 | 13 | (1:27) | 7 | 12 | (1:43) | (1:31) |
| 5 | 9 | 8 | (0:53) | 5 | 9 | (1:48) | 5 | 5 | (1:00) | (1:10) |
| 6 | 14 | 28 | (2:00) | 16 | 26 | (1:39) | 13 | 16 | (1:14) | (1:38) |
| 7 | 24 | 48 | (2:00) | 24 | 39 | (1:38) | 10 | 14 | (1:24) | (1:07) |
| 8 | 9 | 9 | (1:00) | 11 | 14 | (1:16) | 8 | 7 | (0:53) | (1:04) |
| Total | 130 | 263 | (2:01) | 142 | 246 | (1:44) | 103 | 155 | (1:30) | (1:46) |

* Period 2 for ABC included two days not included for other networks: 12/30–31/79; this added seven news reports, and twenty-one minutes.

Table 8.3
Topics Presented by Each Network for Each Period of Observation

| | ABC | | | | | | | | | CBS | | | | | | | | | NBC | | | | | | | | | TOTAL |
|---|---|---|---|---|---|---|---|---|---|---|---|---|---|---|---|---|---|---|---|---|---|---|---|---|---|---|---|---|
| | 1 | 2 | 3 | 4 | 5 | 6 | 7 | 8 | TOTAL | 1 | 2 | 3 | 4 | 5 | 6 | 7 | 8 | TOTAL | 1 | 2 | 3 | 4 | 5 | 6 | 7 | 8 | TOTAL | |
| Hostages | 4 | 6 | 1 | 1 | 0 | 5 | 1 | 2 | (20) | 14 | 12 | 0 | 1 | 0 | 5 | 3 | 1 | (36) | 8 | 7 | 0 | 1 | 1 | 3 | 1 | 0 | (21) | 77 |
| Hostage families | 5 | 3 | 0 | 0 | 0 | 4 | 0 | 0 | (12) | 6 | 2 | 0 | 0 | 0 | 4 | 0 | 0 | (12) | 6 | 0 | 0 | 0 | 0 | 5 | 0 | 0 | (11) | 35 |
| US policies | 4 | 0 | 2 | 0 | 0 | 1 | 0 | 1 | (8) | 5 | 1 | 0 | 0 | 0 | 1 | 0 | 1 | (8) | 4 | 0 | 0 | 0 | 0 | 1 | 0 | 2 | (7) | 23 |
| Shah | 5 | 1 | 2 | 3 | 3[a] | 0 | 0 | 0 | (14) | 9 | 1 | 0 | 4 | 1 | 0 | 0 | 0 | (15) | 9 | 2 | 0 | 2 | 1 | 0 | 0 | 0 | (14) | 43 |
| Iran: | | | | | | | | | | | | | | | | | | | | | | | | | | | | |
| Revolution | 0 | 0 | 0 | 0 | 1 | 0 | 0 | 0 | (1) | 1 | 0 | 1 | 0 | 0 | 0 | 1 | 0 | (3) | 3 | 0 | 0 | 0 | 0 | 0 | 0 | 0 | (3) | 7 |
| Govt. and elections | 0 | 1 | 0 | 2 | 2 | 0 | 1 | 0 | (6) | 0 | 0 | 0 | 0 | 2 | 0 | 0 | 0 | (2) | 0 | 2 | 1 | 1 | 2 | 1 | 2 | 0 | (9) | 17 |
| Islam | 0 | 1 | 0 | 0 | 0 | 0 | 0 | 0 | (1) | 1 | 0 | 1 | 0 | 0 | 0 | 0 | 0 | (2) | 1 | 1 | 0 | 0 | 0 | 0 | 0 | 0 | (2) | 5 |
| External problems[b] | 2 | 4 | 1 | 1 | 0 | 1 | 1 | 8 | (18) | 5 | 3 | 2 | 0 | 1 | 1 | 2 | 3 | (17) | 4 | 4 | 1 | 0 | 1 | 1 | 0 | 3 | (14) | 49 |
| Internal problems[c] | 0 | 0 | 4 | 0 | 0 | 1 | 0 | 0 | (5) | 0 | 2 | 6 | 0 | 0 | 0 | 1 | 0 | (9) | 0 | 3 | 6 | 0 | 0 | 0 | 0 | 0 | (9) | 23 |
| Iranian students in US | 5 | 1 | 0 | 0 | 4 | 0 | 0 | 0 | (10) | 12 | 1 | 0 | 0 | 0 | 1 | 0 | 1 | (15) | 8 | 1 | 0 | 0 | 0 | 0 | 0 | 0 | (9) | 34 |
| United States: | | | | | | | | | | | | | | | | | | | | | | | | | | | | |
| Sanctions | 1 | 6 | 0 | 0 | 0 | 5 | 0 | 0 | (12) | 0 | 2 | 0 | 0 | 0 | 3 | 1 | 0 | (6) | 0 | 1 | 0 | 0 | 0 | 2 | 0 | 0 | (3) | 21 |
| World reaction | 3 | 5 | 4 | 0 | 4 | 5 | 0 | 0 | (21) | 3 | 4 | 0 | 0 | 2 | 3 | 0 | 0 | (12) | 8 | 1 | 1 | 1 | 2 | 3 | 1 | 0 | (17) | 50 |
| Private diplomacy[d] | 0 | 0 | 0 | 0 | 0 | 1 | 0 | 6 | (7) | 1 | 0 | 0 | 0 | 0 | 0 | 0 | 6 | (7) | 0 | 2 | 1 | 0 | 0 | 1 | 0 | 6 | (10) | 24 |
| Economy/oil | 3 | 1 | 0 | 0 | 0 | 2 | 0 | 0 | (6) | 5 | 0 | 0 | 0 | 0 | 2 | 0 | 0 | (7) | 4 | 0 | 0 | 0 | 0 | 0 | 0 | 0 | (4) | 17 |
| Rescue attempt | 0 | 0 | 0 | 0 | 0 | 0 | 14 | 1 | (15) | 0 | 0 | 0 | 0 | 0 | 0 | 11 | 1 | (12) | 0 | 0 | 0 | 0 | 0 | 0 | 7 | 1 | (8) | 35 |

[a] Analysis of reports for ABC between 3/23–31/80 showed that 22 reports pertained to the Shah.

[b] Includes reports about Iraq, Afghanistan, problems with the Soviet Union.

[c] Mainly refers to ethnic and regional disputes.

[d] Private diplomacy, mainly by members of hostages' families, although the cases in period 8 pertain to Ramsey Clark's and others' efforts.

137

and so forth. Seven reports directly pertained to his health and ensuing operations. However, during the dates of this study, only nine reports about the Shah's history as a ruler were presented. These few were prompted by inquiries of the United Nations commission visiting Iran (period four). In other words, there was more news emphasis on virtually all other topics examined in this study than on the history of Iran under the Shah.[4]

Iran's Foreign Minister, Sadegh Ghotbzadeh, was perplexed by this brand of news coverage. He said on the *MacNeil/Lehrer Report* (November 29, 1979:

> Well, we want the Shah. You always forget the problem of the Shah. You never *talk* about the Shah, you never talk about his crimes. Why don't you do that from time to time? If the lives and the safety and the comfort of the forty-nine Americans is so important to you all, why is it not important for you to look around and see what one nation has [been] submitted [to] in the past twenty-five years? Why don't you look at *that* a little bit?

The Shah of Iran, on the whole, received what could be termed "favorable" television coverage, mainly due to what was omitted from the reports. Since the official government position was that the Shah had been a friend of the United States, that our humanitarian policies opened our hospital doors to this ailing fallen monarch, and that under no circumstances was the taking of hostages justified, the history and the future of the Shah were irrelevant to official US policy. Stated differently, numerous reports emphasized that the Iranian interest in returning the Shah to Iran was irrelevant to the hostage situation, as were past indiscretions of the US government. Such matters, the argument ran, could be discussed at a later date, following the release of the hostages. This view was implicitly if not explicitly reflected in the news reports scrutinized during these periods.

Favorable reporting of the Shah is nothing new. William A. Dorman and Ehsan Omeed's (1979) provocative essay, "Reporting Iran the Shah's Way," documented the misinformed coverage of the events in Iran leading up to the revolution in 1978 and subsequent developments in 1979. They concluded that the reporting was quite compatible with the views of the administration toward any "unsettling" influences in the Mideast—especially toward the dictatorship in Iran which Western dollars had buttressed with military power, industrialization, and a Western notion of progress and lifestyle that was hardly commensurate with the deep-rooted cultural and religious traditions of Islam. Then, as in early 1980, the Shah represented Western consciousness in speech, dress, manner, and major values, although

---

[4] This is not to say that there were no negative stories about the Shah on television. For example, on March 3, 1980, CBS's *60 Minutes* devoted some forty minutes of critical reporting to the Shah, including his American support.

many who support such notions would not go along with the brutal means his secret police, SAVAK, used to implement programs and policies. But the media, with the exception of certain reports about brutal practices of enforcement, seldom reflected on the activities of the Shah.

Given this context for the hostage crisis, reports tended to focus on themes compatible with the U.S. position. The logic imposed by the West, though unaccepted by the religious leaders of the emergent government, was that international law should be followed faithfully, that it had been followed during the Shah's regime, and that the revolutionary government was, in effect, an accomplice in its breach. Numerous reports followed about "civilized" countries condemning Iran through the United Nations and the International Court of Justice and demanding the hostages' release. All of this further cemented the image of lawless Moslems acting above the law, barbaric if not stupid.

A few journalists avoided the standard "legalistic" orientation, or the empty "updating" of the hostage status. They sometimes attempted to give some empathic understanding of what was going on. One such person was George Lewis of NBC. When asked if he felt the Iranians are "crazy" or whether "they have a justification for that anger?," Lewis replied:

> I think I've come to understand the depth of their feeling over my two months in Iran. Remember the scene with Kurt Waldheim and the people who were mutilated, and there was a little boy in the audience there. His arms had been chopped off. We were told that that boy had been tortured by SAVAK, the Shah's secret police, in the presence of his father. They were trying to obtain a confession from his father, and when you see pictures like that, when you talk to people who have lost family members to the Shah's secret police, you begin to understand the depth of their emotion (1/16/81, NBC, Special Report, "Crisis in Iran: 1 Year After the Shah," 11:30 PM)

Such views seldom found their way to the prime time newscasts. More typical of what was presented is illustrated by NBC's Richard Valeriani's report of the "situation room" at the State Department on November 5, 1979:

> There's a tremendous sense of frustration here and elsewhere at the department because of the poor communications with Tehran, because of the chaotic political situation there, and because of the difficulty in trying to deal with people who ignore normal diplomatic practices.

## ISLAM IN IRAN

Table 8.3 presents the number of stories focusing on several aspects of Iranian life and politics. It seems paradoxical that Islam, perhaps the most relevant context for understanding the political situation in Iran, received so little coverage. While the religious-cultural relationship in Iran cannot be explicated in this study, even a cursory glance at history, scholarly accounts, and casual comments of Iranian citizens reveals that the role of religion and spirituality is quite distinct from that of the Western world. The way Westerners are accustomed to viewing politically relevant matters is to think in certain geopolitical terms, strongly enmeshed in a logic that puts decision-making on a secular-ideological basis. Thus, educated Americans have, in general, come to think of conflicts between countries within an ideologically defined framework, e.g., capitalism, communism, socialism, or nonaligned. That this has a distinctive economic cast to it comes as no surprise given the coterminous relationship in most societies between various dimensions of economic power and political power. Yet, the Iranian revolution had emerged into a movement by some religious leaders to engulf the state within the societal-religious orientation, and this was something that the United States not only did not support, but in a certain sense, either never understood or refused to accept. This view was especially true on network newscasts.

Television news lacked systematic coverage of religion in Iran. One ABC Special Report (12/7/79) devoted three and one-half minutes to the history of Islam and its role in Iran, but the extent of the complex intermingling between "church" and "state" was lost in favor of simplistic Western-oriented comparisons. One reporter explained the term "Ayatollah" as an equivalent to "excellency," but with religious overtones.

By way of contrast, newscasts and special reports analyzed in this study contained nothing as extensive as the following statements made by Professor Bernard Lewis, a specialist in Near Eastern Studies, Princeton University, months earlier on the *MacNeil/Lehrer Report* (February 8, 1979):

> Islam as such is obviously a religion. But I think when one uses the word "religion" one has to distinguish; religion doesn't mean the same thing to all peoples. And Islam from its very inception has been much more closely involved with the conduct of government than has Christianity or Judaism... from the very beginnings of Islam, the formative years of the Islamic religion, there has been an intimate association between religion and government, [involving] the exercise of power, which is lacking in the other religions with which we are familiar... church and state are one and the same. There aren't two separate institutions which could be separated.... In ideal Islam, and in a good deal of Islamic history, they are one and the same. So the question of a separation between them doesn't arise.

Other *MacNeil/Lehrer Reports* were also on target. On November 17, 1978, nearly one year before the United States embassy was overrun, Shahriar Rouhani, an associate of the Ayatollah Khomeini and a Ph.D. candidate at Yale University, told Robert MacNeil:

...the aim of the struggle is toward establishment of an Islamic government. Islamic government may sound extremely alien, which is
very natural. In fact—especially as far as the comparison with Saudi
Arabia or... Libya is concerned—none of those countries are Islamic.
We want an Islamic government which naturally ensures the full freedom and participation of the people.

Khomeini's vision of a just society commensurate with centuries of Islamic
thought was founded on "the regulation of man's relationship to man for
the attainment of man's mortal happiness" (Ismael & Ismael, 1980:616).
Khomeini says of Westerners and those who are Westernized:

... they are still backward in the sphere of securing happiness to man,
backward in spreading moral virtues and backward in creating a
psychological and spiritual progress similar to the material progress.
They are still unable to solve their social problems because solving
these problems and eliminating hardship requires an ideological and
moral spirit (quoted in Ismael & Ismael, 1980:616).

These points of emphasis were hardly understood by the American press,
and certainly not appreciated.

Ayatollah Khomeini and the Islamic orientation he represented were
the subject of ridicule and derision throughout the period of this study. In
one of the few "comments" labeled as such by journalists, David Brinkley
claimed that the Ayatollah Khomeini was simply out of touch with reality,
that there was no religious war, that there was no ill feeling toward Islam
in the United States, and that the real issue was that the West had tried to
plunder Iran and failed, but Iran was succeeding in doing it to the United
States. After deriding Khomeini further, Brinkley concluded by asking,
"How can the United States deal with a man whose thoughts seem frozen
somewhere in about the tenth century?" (NBC, 12/26/79)

Numerous news reporters referred to Khomeini as eccentric and
mysterious, while one stated he was certifiable as "nuts" (ABC, 4/25/80). In
commentary by CBS's Rod Macleish, the message of an anachronistic man
with weird ideas is apparent (11/10/79):

Khomeini has been feuding with the now departed government of
Mehdi Bazargan, a Western-oriented moderate who wanted to solve
Iran's problems with technology and efficiency, while the Ayatollah's
primary drive is to return Iran to seventh century Islamic principles.

At the core of the problem of press treatment was that Iran was neither
East nor West, neither capitalist nor communist; apparently the only viable
option was to see their avowed religious and political orientation as "weird,"
"crazy," and unpredictable. Anyone who would follow such fanatic leadership also had to be a zealot, devoid of any rationality. George Ball, former
undersecretary of State, put it this way:

But you have to understand that this man is a fanatic. . . he necessarily plays a very dangerous game, because he thinks in terms which are totally incomprehensible to Western minds. (NBC, Special Report: Crisis in Iran: The Turmoil Spreads, 11/26/79)

As though this idea needed to be further reinforced, NBC's John Chancellor said in his closing remarks:

Everybody but the Ayatollah and his fanatic followers would like to disown the whole thing; but the problem is that this crisis is far from the stage where it can be diffused.

## FAMILIES OF HOSTAGES

Another periodic focus of coverage was the views and emotional states of families of the hostages. The family reaction, while most heavily hit during the initial months of captivity, was always available for a feature story on holidays, or for a quick reaction to a move by the White House or by the Iranians. Holiday stories were particularly noteworthy since one or more family members could be shown on film to be crying, or emotionally drained. With so many of the news reports stemming from officialdom, stories about families afforded journalists an opportunity to do some reporting on a slightly less routine aspect of the hostage story. (The self-proclaimed role of at least one network, ABC, to console Americans over the hostage situation was apparent when the Christmas Eve newscast presented nearly five minutes of Luciano Pavarotti singing "Ave Maria.")

Coverage was not randomly distributed over all the loved ones of the imprisoned hostages, however. During the periods of this study, three or four families received more attention than the others. A general profile of media prominent families suggests that they tended to be articulate, clearly supportive of the administration's efforts to free the hostages, or openly critical—even defiantly so, as in the case of Mr. and Mrs. Timm, parents of Kevin Hermining, in their independent efforts to free their son by traveling to Tehran and by criticizing President Carter's approach.

Coverage of the hostages and the families was often combined, especially during holiday periods, but also following interviews with hostages. The first televised interview was on December 10, 1979; two NBC reporters questioned Corporal William Gallegos of Pueblo, Colorado. The interview had been split into three segments, each one followed by comments from one or more reporters interviewing each other, officials, or Corporal Gallego's parents, who watched the interview in the NBC affiliate studio in Denver, Colorado. Gallegos' parents were permitted to make only a few comments—about one page out of a total program transcript of forty-three pages—but they were nonetheless placed in the format of the program. That they may have had deep personal feeling which they may not have wished to share with a national TV audience, or perhaps were unable to articulate how they felt, was not a relevant consideration.

Throughout this period, a number of the families involved were apparently willing and eager to appear on television. Perhaps the most extreme reverence for a television appearance occurred on ABC's *Nightline* on April 25, 1980, the day of the unsuccessful rescue attempt. The parents of one of the soldiers killed in this mission, Corporal George Holmes, Jr., were being interviewed on the air live by Ted Koppel. Following his question as to why they agreed to be interviewed, Mrs. Holmes replied: "We feel no ill will or no grudges against anyone." The dead soldier's mother then asked Koppel's permission to hand the microphone to her husand who also made some comments about his son.

## IRANIAN STUDENTS IN THE US

News coverage of Iranian students in the United States was concentrated in the first observational period. More media attention was given to this topic (34 reports) than to the revolution, Islam, or the elections. Iranian students in the US were of special interest for four reasons: first, they were in this country and spoke English; second, they were involved in good film stories involving demonstrations and often violent clashes; third, they were the targets of governmental "tough action" to deport those students who were violating immigration guidelines; finally, Iranian students became a symbolic target for American retaliation against Iran. Thus, the "enemy" was brought home and challenged.

Three major angles were stressed in reports about Iranians studying in the United States: the number of them, their hostility toward the Shah, and American reactions to their presence in the country. Before the embassy takeover, network news had featured demonstrating Iranian students in Beverly Hills in January, 1978, protesting the presence of the Shah's sister in the United States. Footage of these confrontations with police and others were shown several times again in November, 1979. But Americans were not very interested in such Iranian activities until the hostages were taken.

Along with reports of the taking of American hostages came film of Iranians demonstrating at the Statue of Liberty against the presence of the Shah, who was in New York for medical treatment. Moreover, newscasts often showed crowds of demonstrators in Iran and then immediately switched to film of Iranians demonstrating in the United States. Reports were broadcast that as many as 50,000 Iranians were studying in the United States. As the visibility of Iranian student demonstrations in the US became joined to the problems in Iran, it was no surprise that Americans began engaging in counterdemonstrations in a handful of cities throughout the United States. Statements by some Congressmen were aired on NBC on November 7, 1979, requesting the deportation of those students who demonstrated at the Statue of Liberty on November 4. ABC's and CBS's November 7 evening newscasts featured Iranian students in Houston demonstrating in support of the Ayatollah Khomeini. By November 8, American citizens became more actively involved when an Iranian flag was destroyed in front of the Iranian consulate in Houston. CBS's report of this demonstration included an interview with a man wearing a cowboy hat and baseball undershirt. In response to the question, "do you think Carter is doing enough?" he replied:

> I think it speaks for itself...I think negotiation time is over with. I think he is fairly afraid to send the US forces there. I'm a former Marine, I think he should take a detachment of Marines, or just give us 50 Texans or 50 cowboys, and we'll go over there and take care of the situation.

Throughout these initial reports and throughout those that followed during the next two months, several themes were consistently used:

1.  Iranian students in this country were in complete agreement on their support of Khomeini, the taking of hostages, and their dislike for the Shah
2.  Support for Khomeini and the revolution was the same as support for the taking of hostages
3.  These students blamed all American citizens

Consistent with network news coverage of this complex situation, very few interviews were conducted with Iranian students to get their views. However, on November 8, ABC's John Lawrence interviewed four Iranian students at the University of Southern California. One stated that the taking of hostages was not right and that he disagreed with it; another explained that this was done in retaliation for letting the Shah into the United States. When the interviewer asked why the United States should not respond by holding them hostages, as some in Congress had suggested, one student replied: "The United States is a civilized country...with educated people, and being educated people, I very much doubt they would do such a thing."

Film of the Iranian struggles with police some months earlier in Beverly Hills was shown prior to the interviewees' replies. The report ended by referring to a disturbance that had occurred on campus, but nobody had been hurt.

The next day, November 9, CBS covered the following anti-Iranian violence and activity throughout the United States: fighting had broken out in Beverly Hills; scuffling had occurred at the University of Washington in Seattle; 13,000 had demonstrated in Washington, D.C.; an effigy of the Ayatollah Khomeini had been hanged at the University of Colorado; a snowball fight had been waged between pro and anti-Khomeini students at the University of Minnesota; and anti-Iranian activity had occurred in Springfield, Massachusetts.

Film of these confrontations contained some of the most brutal, vivid film ever seen by this investigator: people from angry crowds were shown attacking greatly outnumbered Iranian students. Extremist sentiments were highlighted. For example, one man was shown yelling, "I'm sick of getting stomped on; we're not going to take it anymore, America!" Behind this man were several black Americans also denouncing Iranian students. The reporter closed this piece by noting that one demonstrator was heard to say, as a bleeding Iranian was led away, "more blood, more blood."

Along with these reports of anti-Iranian sentiment, and the vivid beatings presented at prime time, there was also the subtle message that police officers were not going to tolerate the Iranian student demonstrations. In nearly every report presented, such as the one from Beverly Hills, it was noted that most of these arrested were Iranians (140 of 155 in the case of Beverly Hills). Nothing was said by any of the reporters about the irony or fairness of all of this. To the contrary, the suggestion was that this was somehow inevitable and perhaps sanctioned. Senator Jackson was shown on NBC's evening newscast (11/19/79) saying: "If the Iranian students continue to demonstrate against the United States government and in favor of what is going on in Tehran, I believe that this can lead to some rather drastic responses on the part of the American people."

Finally, on November 10, 1979, it was reported that Iranian students not in complete compliance with immigration guidelines would be deported. Only CBS's reporter, Fred Graham, in an exceptional piece of reporting, attempted to give some perspective on this move. He noted that it was really a message to Iranian students to cease their demonstrations, and that the State Department could not cite another instance where a particular group was singled out to scrutinize their compliance with immigration rules.

The next day, Graham continued his exemplary work by getting reactions from the American Civil Liberties Union, noting that most Iranian students in this country were simply trying to study, and indeed, were not so politically active. Two students were interviewed, and they stressed that they had already spent considerable sums of money and time on their studies, and they did not think it was fair that they might have to leave.

So vivid were the news reports about anti-Iranian sentiment, that Rod Macleish devoted an entire commentary to the treatment of Iranians in the United States. After noting it is as idiotic to blame Iranians in the United

States for what is going on in Iran as it is to blame Americans in Iran for US policy there, he added:

> In Iran all seems to have collapsed. Authority is invested in the whims of a mysterious old man. In American we've tried as a basic principle to restrain ourselves by placing the law above the passions of any particular moment. . . . In this country, an Iranian student, whatever his political beliefs, has rights, because the law says he does. (CBS News, 11/11/79)

This commentary is particularly unusual because no reports were aired about violations of rights of Iranian students, even though it was reported by NBC on November 9 that the FBI had infiltrated Iranian student groups for the past three years and was turning over information about individuals to officials. The reporter, Carl Stern, who also has a law degree and who was heavily involved in coverage of clandestine activities by the Justice Department during Nixon's terms in office, said nothing critical of this. He did not further examine exactly what the FBI had done, or ask if rights had been violated or if the FBI had overstepped its bounds. The network moved directly to the next report.

The upshot of these patterns is that Iranian students (along with the hostage families) were singled out as the "domestic" side of the hostage story. Network coverage consisted mostly of demonstration and confrontations, rather than, for example, the multiple perspectives of Iranian students studying in the United States, their particular problems, or the nature of financial, employment, and even law enforcement discrimination against them. Rather, they were treated, on the whole, as a unified quasi-army that would like to do to the United States at home what their "counterparts" were doing to American hostages in Iran.

## NEWS SOURCES

The complexity of the issues and context of the American hostage story demanded, if it were to be told accurately, an understanding of the motives, character, and background of leaders and followers alike in both countries. The journalistic enterprise to do this kind of investigation was limited not by the amount of time available over the course of many months of reporting, but was limited by the continued reliance on officials as news sources. Reporters commonly turned to those officials having a Western appearance who also spoke English, rather than seeking out their more indigenous-appearing and speaking counterparts. The frequency with which selected individuals and officials appeared in network newsfilm is presented in Table 8.4.

**Table 8.4**
**Total Network Film Presentations of Officials and Others**
**Interviewed in Iran and the United States\***

| Iran | | United States | |
|------|------|------|------|
| Individual | Frequency | Individual | Frequency |
| Ghotbzadeh | 16 | Pres. Carter | 10 |
| Bandi-Sadr | 5 | Hodding Carter | 21 |
| A. Khomeini | 13 | Jody Powell | 6 |
| A. Beheshti | 11 | Cyrus Vance | 5 |
| A. Shariat-Madari | 2 | Z. Brzezinski | 2 |
| other rel. leaders | 7 | Harold Brown | 1 |
| "militants" | 6 | Tom Reston | 4 |
| other officials | 12 | Senators/Congressmen | 9 |
| nonofficials | 2 | other officials | 20 |
| | | nonofficials | 21 |
| | | clergy | 6 |

\* Cases are included when the person appeared on camera for at least 10 seconds, even if a reporter was not able to ask questions. In some instances, an interpreter's voice, or a reporter's "voice-over" was heard.

Network focus on United States government reactions to statements or events by Iranians and others accounts for most of the tabulations presented in Table 8.4. With only a few exceptions, network reporters would attend either White House, State Department, or Congressional press conferences or interview one or more of these officials to get their reaction. Their questions often sought reactions to something another official mentioned in a prior press conference. Disagreements with these American officials seldom occurred. In the periods of observation of this study, there was not one serious disagreement or harsh exchange between a journalist and a US official. Things were different for Iranian interviewees.

Like their American counterparts, Iranian officials dominated network appearances, but they tended to be treated as adversaries, and in some cases as outright enemies. Sadegh Ghotbzadeh, Iran's Foreign Minister and former head of Iranian Radio and Television, was interviewed and shown sixteen times in the periods of this study, compared to five times for President Bani-Sadr, who, while having a Western appearance, did not speak English. Ayatollah Khomeini was shown speaking thirteen times, through an interpreter, or as the reporter provided a "voice over" film and gave a summary of what was being said. The other most frequently appearing Ayatollah, Mohammed Behesti, was shown eleven times. He was dressed like the other religious leaders, but he did speak English.

Only twice were nonofficials shown speaking, through an interpreter or otherwise. This is no surprise because, to this investigator's knowledge, none of the network journalists spoke Farsi. They would have had trouble communicating with Iranian citizens who did not speak English. Nevertheless, this omission from news reports indicates a general lack of interest in obtaining the perspective from Iranian citizens. As discussed later, however, American audiences did receive impressions of Iranian citizens from the ubiquitous film reports of crowds.

Unable to speak Farsi, unfamiliar with Iranian customs, and perhaps uneasy in their perceived role as supporters of the US government position, broadcast journalists tended to see Iranian officials as adversaries who wanted to use them for propaganda purposes. One consequence was to see most statements, along with film or interview opportunities, as propaganda efforts which could be either ignored, or, if accepted, done so grudgingly with clear reminders that the journalists were aware of the "hidden" message and motive.

This tact was perhaps most apparent during an interview between ABC's Barry Serafin (12/28/79) and "Habib" and "Mary," two spokespersons for the students holding the hostages. After "Mary" preceded answers to several of Serafin's questions about the hostages with political statements promoting the students' position and their faith in the Ayatollah Khomeini, Serafin sternly instructed her to give just a simple "yes" or "no" answer to the question. Such conditions were never imposed on Western officials who inserted self-serving statements prior to—or instead of—answering reporters' questions. Moreover, Serafin appeared to take a certain amount of pleasure in reporting that at the conclusion of the interview, the two interviewees got up and stormed out of the station saying the interviewer had been rude.

## VISUAL IMAGES FROM IRAN

Though Americans learned little about the government personnel who were taken hostage, the network newscasts contributed immeasurably to a generalized image of Americans as hostages and of all Iranians as their captors. These images came mainly through photos, logos, graphics, and film. ABC's photo-logo of blindfolded hostage Jerry Miele provided a compelling reminder of the fact that hostages were still being held over the months and also suggested something about their treatment.

Another reminder was the film of Barry Rosen being paraded, along with other hostages, before the predominately American news media. Like other press conferences and clergy visits, it was a media phenomenon, geared to visual representations which would be broadcast internationally (Heumann, 1980). This film, like footage of similar dramatizations would be repeated whenever the hostage situation was "reviewed" by the media at regular intervals, such as 100 days, 300 days, and so forth. This particular filmed presentation of the hostages, lasting only a few minutes, assumed a life of its own and reinforced a certain image of how the hostages were being treated, even though reports by former hostages and most letters to families indicated that this episode was not typical.

Another primary visual image in hundreds of news reports over the following months was the American embassy in Tehran. Not surprisingly, the crowd activities occuring there became a standard visual part of the days' coverage, regardless of its immediate relevance to the news of the day. On several occasions, following a brief report that nothing had changed with the hostages, film of demonstrators would be shown as the reporter discussed comments or action by one or more members of the revolutionary committee. In this way, the crowds at the embassy became formatted as part of the Iranian coverage. (File film of crowds was later used when crowds did not assemble and following the expulsion of American journalists from Iran.) The effect was to join visually the American hostages, the American embassy, and the chanting crowds.

One consequence of this visual emphasis was to further compound an already strange encounter with adversaries from a different culture with a different worldview and a very different religion. What was seldom shown, for example, were representations of routine life in Iran and what Islam involves on a day-to-day basis. Media personnel were not unaware of this tendency, although the push to deliver exciting film and to maintain the "story" on the embassy created such a distorted view of Iran that little attention was given to the context in which the hostage situation emerged.

A revealing exchange took place between Garrick Utley and George Lewis on January 16, 1980, during an NBC Special Report:

> UTLEY: What is happening there? Do Americans really understand what is happening there?
>
> LEWIS: I think, Garrick, that the impression we convey [is] from the scenes in front of the embassy: all the fist shakers yelling "Death to Carter, Death to America." We conveyed a picture of a nation in the grip of madness, and yet just a few blocks away from the embassy gates people are going about their lives in a normal fashion. Mothers are taking their babies to the park. Businesses are opened. Tehran is pretty much working as normal.

Indeed, the routine presentation on newscasts of chanting and demonstrating crowds with signs in English gave the impression that Iranians must prefer crowds and spend most of their time in the vicinity of the American embassy. The overwhelming message of news film was that these people had little else to think about or do. Iranian students in the United States were presented in a similar way.

Of reports from Tehran, only a handful of presentations involving Iranian subjects did not feature crowd demonstration activities: 3 of 24 for ABC; 6 of 28 for CBS; 6 of 23 for NBC. For film or tape presentations of Iranians in the United States, the discrepancy was even greater. Except for two interviews by ABC in November, for the periods of this study, there were no film stories of Iranian students engaging in routine activities. However, there were thirteen film reports showing these students engaging in demonstrations.

The emphasis on crowd action, or "mob scene" as some journalists referred to it, did not always please Iranian officials, who were interested in portraying a more favorable image of Iranian citizens and of the emergent revolutionary government. Partly for this reason, the revolutionary government took steps to remove foreign journalists from certain countries, including the United States, in early January, 1980. Liz Trotta, a reporter for CBS, interviewed Sadegh, the press liaison official for foreign journalists, about the reasoning behind expulsion of most foreign journalists. His claim that "negative reporting" about Iran was distorting the reality of Iranian life was given but a small place in the report. His major point that other routine dimensions of everyday life in Iran were overlooked, was likewise deemphasized.

In what follows, the text of the report and the film being shown are presented in order to illustrate how the organization of this report, ostensibly attempting to put the news coverage in focus, really ended up creating the same impression that Sadegh was criticizing in the first place. In a report on media problems in presenting cultural differences, that lasted two-minutes and thirty seconds, only about twenty seconds were used to visually present daily life:

| Statement | Visual |
| --- | --- |
| TROTTA: There are about 150 foreign newsmen in Iran now. They come from all over the world to cover this major story, and are permitted to work after they are accredited by the Ministry of National Guidance. | journalists and cameras |
| For the most part, journalists here have been accorded the freedom of movement they enjoy in Western countries. But now that freedom is threatened by an announcement from the government that Western journalists may be expelled from Iran in the near future. | Ghotzbadeh and journalists walking |
| SADEGH: Our revolution has created a vast cultural gap—from what the West understands life should be, and we're trying to close this gap and this is where the media can help a great deal. | Sadegh sitting behind his desk |

| Statement | Visual |
| --- | --- |
| TROTTA: Indeed, there is a culture gap. The very nature and ritual of Islam is an intellectual confrontation for the West. And the new religious militancy inspired by the revolution has only heightened the challenge. | film of crowds, self-flagellation, mass praying |
| As with most stories, there are negative aspects in the telling of the Iran story: bloody challenges to the Khomeini government in one province; the mistrust and defiance of the new regime in another province, | crowd, chanting and waving knives, weapons<br><br>people running |
| a serious threat to Ayatollah Khomeini. From an official point of view, the Western press focuses too closely on these aspects. | man holding a gun; closeup of a man peering through wrap around face; man on roof with gun; crowd |
| SADEGH: When I have an American reporter from one of the major television stations coming from Rome, and he says, "My God, I thought the whole country was falling apart. I was even afraid of how I am going to get from the airport to the hotel, and then I came and I saw everything calm and quiet. I was surprised." That reflects the kind of negative reporting, or reporting out of context. | |
| TROTTA: In the midst of these political and religious clashes, there is a semblance of normalcy in the city of Tehran. The legendary traffic jams are still a game of nerve and skill; the businessmen and housewives maintain the daily life; street vendors cook their hot red beets in the markets. | vendors; autos; woman making purchase from street vendor; beets cooking; people walking; crowd; burning flag; chanting crowd |
| But against this background, one must weigh the headlines: Afghans attack the Soviet embassy in Tehran; Armenians attack the Turkish embassy in Tehran; Afghans attack the Afghanistan embassy in Tehran; and above all, Americans still captive in the US embassy. | chains on embassy gate; camera pointed at embassy |
| Liz Trotta, CBS News, Tehren. | |

This is one of the longest segments that was broadcast during the period under study that was devoted to "routine activity" in Iran.

## TELEVISION DIPLOMACY

Television's role went beyond merely bringing the sad faces and tears of hostage families into the homes of millions of Americans. Television also became the dominant forum for negotiation and diplomacy, largely because the Iranians, like the US government, made considerable effort to join public relations to foreign policy. As *Washington Post* correspondent

Don Oberdorfer said about the media's role in Iran on the *MacNeil/Lehrer Report* (December 12, 1979):

> In some ways television is almost the essence of this crisis. . . . We have two contending parties that are trading blows by wars of words, and the primary objective on the part of those holding the hostages in the American Embassy in Tehran is to make a change in the mind of the American public about what the American government must do, with the Shah, with national policy, in all kinds of ways. They're also trying to reach out, through communications means, to the rest of the world, especially the Third World. . . We in this country and our government have been completely tied up really for more than five weeks with this matter. There is no physical threat to fifty Americans. But it's a completely different sort of thing than the usual international crisis of armies marching or missiles on the ready and so on, and it's really all about this kind of war of opinion.

This role of television diplomacy was explicitly referred to during NBC's discussion of the interview with Corporal Gallegos. The following exchange occurred between moderator Garrick Utley and reporter Ford Rowan:

> ROWAN: Some officials say that it will be harder to find a remedy to win the hostages' release now. They say prime time TV exposure for the students' spokesmen and for their handpicked hostage may lead the students to believe that they are winning their effort to influence American public opinion and that time is on their side.
>
> UTLEY: Ford, as press secretary Powell intimated just a moment ago, they were not at the White House very happy to see this in prime time and yet television has been *the* principle means of communicating information in this whole story over the past five weeks.
>
> ROWAN: You are absolutely right that there has been a breakdown in traditional diplomacy. . . —the conduit [for information] has been— the news media. [People in Washington] are pouring over this interview to find out any clues they can and to try to piece together the information that has come from Tehran. . . But the criticism comes from the people who believe that the American media. . . has been manipulated by the Iranian officials and the so-called students, and that we have played into their hand and in effect sold out to them. . . . They are guessing that there will be continuing efforts to manipulate the American news media and that you will see more PR from Iran and that it probably will escalate in the days ahead.

As stressed throughout this paper, television news was integrally involved with both Iranian and American diplomatic motions. And the media people clearly took this to heart, accepting this responsibility which no one had given to them. For example, just prior to the Rowan Utley exchange, Utley had asked White House Press Secretary Jody Powell if

Gallegos were trying to communicate a secret message. Powell replied (November 19, 1979):

> Well, Garrick, I detected no secret message, and I think it's quite clear that, had we been able to do so, the worst thing we could do would be to say so on television.

The role of TV news in particular had already been accepted in this crisis, largely because of the growing emergence of a tie between the logic and relevance of the mass media and numerous other aspects of daily life, including foreign policy and international communication. Most reporters saw no difficulty in TV diplomacy—although others would disavow that this was in fact taking place. Indeed, the reporters who interviewed Gallegos clearly illustrate the role of the journalist as observer, information gatherer, and broadly informed communicator who could clarify and straighten out ambiguous twists on complex issues and events; in addition, reports in the present study tended to support administration practices and "viable options."

During the Gallegos interview, an NBC reporter took issue with this hostage of five weeks who suggested that perhaps the Shah was not a "good cause" for him to continue being held captive. The interviewer said: "Let me ask you one other question. If President Carter accedes to the demand that the Shah be returned, isn't that inviting similar attacks on other US embassies elsewhere in the world? Isn't that saying to the world, in effect, you want something from America, just occupy one of our embassies and take a few hostages?"

As the foregoing suggests, broadcast journalists tended to support the administration's general view and approach. In some instances, however, reporters mentioned possible tougher actions, such as a military option, before any official publicly discussed it. ABC's Sam Donaldson, for example, concluded a report on November 8, 1979, just four days after the embassy takeover, by saying:

> Notwithstanding such constraint, it is understood here and ought to be understood in Iran, that, if any harm does come to the Americans, the president will not hesitate to order an appropriate American military response.

This pronouncement and the gusto with which it was offered implied that Donaldson agreed with this scenario. More importantly, it was not at all clear whether this was a White House "off the record" appraisal or the reporter's own warning. Just two days after the embassy takeover, on November 6, 1979, CBS' Marvin Kalb observed, "Resorting to force won't save lives, and sticking with diplomacy isn't getting the hostages out either." He then paraphrased what one official had said as part of his closing remarks. "This is getting to be a national humiliation, and there is no way out yet."

## CONCLUSION

The major television networks played a central role in the definition and presentation of the history, nature, and consequences of the hostage situation in Iran. Despiite network disclaimers to the contrary, there can be no question that decisions to emphasize certain events, individuals, and themes had a bearing on the character of developments in Iran. Despite the obvious manner in which international diplomacy became wedded to regular newscasts, no claim is being made that television prolonged the crisis or could have prevented it from happening. Yet, public impressions and resultant "opinion poll" messages to political leaders here and abroad were clearly important ingredients in the Iranian situation. Exactly what those effects have been awaits further research, and will of necessity require further content analyses and extensive interviewing with relevent officials.

Of critical value in this study is the clarification of the role of television news throughout the coverage of these events. For the most part, broadcast journalists were advocates, surrogate diplomats, and occasionally the "devil's advocate" for governmental initiatives and policies. With the exception of some instances cited previously, one seldom finds examples of independent investigation or alternative ways of interpreting events. To the contrary, network correspondents tended to be spokespersons for State Department and other governmental officials, providing what amounted to a unified "policy" of selection, interpretation, and presentation of information.

There were some instances of journalistic reflection on reporting procedures and obvious limitations. Most of these segments originated from Iran, involved dependence on Iranian officials who were not always cooperative, and often involved matters of censorship. Mostly during the first three observational periods, twelve such reports were presented about problems of censorship—chiefly about Iranian officials denying access to interviews, or cutting off transmitting power and other technological necessities of television broadcasting. However, even in the reports where journalists attempted to evaluate and assess the impact of their reporting, essentially none of the points raised in this essay were mentioned. One reason is that journalists seldom keep track of reports over time, especially those of colleagues. As a consequence, facts in those stories are no longer relevant to a current report. What is recalled instead is the ongoing story line or "theme," the unifying "big picture" which permits journalists to join one report to another over a period of several days, weeks, and, in this case, even months. The potential distorting influences of this practice on subsequent reports is a troublesome issue that few journalists have seriously examined (cf. Altheide, 1980).

The organization of television does impose certain limitations on what is likely to be presented and in the depth of reporting. Broadcast journalists often defend superficial but very entertaining reports by saying that they do not have the time to study, evaluate, and thoroughly understand complex events and by noting that those events are to be presented within a time frame of one or two minutes. Coverage of the Iranian situation raises serious questions about this standard defense for poor reporting. Because the episode continued for so long, reporters and network staffs had literally months to familiarize themselves with the intricacies of Iran and of past American policies and also had many dozens of hours of news stories in which to distill these matters. On the whole, this was not done. Network news is prepared according to formats; and in the case of Iran, formats were developed to further accomodate the established practices.

The ABC late evening newscast, *Crisis in Iran*, was a regularly scheduled newscast which was originally intended to be devoted mainly to Iran, but it evolved into *Nightline* on March 24 and quickly turned to other topics as well. The format of this show involved live interviews with officials, experts, and other concerned people about a varietyof topics. In the case of Iran, ABC might have an Iranian official, such as Foreign Minister Sadegh Ghotzbadeh, on one telephone, with a member of the hostage's family or a US official on another telephone. The moderator, Ted Koppel, may ask each questions and they could also ask each other questions. Such a format is superior to the short and visual film reports characteristic of regular network newscasts, although even this approach tended to evolve into argumentation rather than clarification, putting the reporter on center stage, and generally presenting the administration's position. Perhaps not surprisingly, even after months of such reports, the journalists involved evidenced little detectable change, expertise, or sense of perspective, although they did appear to become more frustrated.

The Iranian situation was reduced to one story—the freeing of the hostages—rather than coverage of its background and context, of the complexities of Iran, of alternative American policies, and of contemporary parochial politics in a world dominated by superpowers. Such messages were not forthcoming in the face of counts of the number of days of captivity and more footage of angry demonstrators and emotional relatives of hostages. That was part of the story, but, as this chapter has suggested, that was not the only story.

Like it or not, the typical American citizen's understanding of contemporary affairs, especially international events, depends more and more on television news. Americans will be better informed only if people in the media choose to reflect on the character of coverage of specific events over time, to consider seriously criticism and suggestions, and, when warranted, to act on these reflections. Otherwise, it will not be true that 'the more you watch the more you know." To the contrary, the opposite may occur—well-informed ignorance. As Garrick Utley reminded Americans in the context of another message (11/12/79, NBC, "Crisis in Iran: The US Responds"):

> This could go on for a long time. It will be a time of continuing tension and anger. Above all, it is a time for clear minds and clear heads.

## REFERENCES

Altheide, David L. 1976. *Creating Reality: How TV News Distorts Events*. Beverly Hills, Calif.: Sage.

———· 1980. Learning from Mistakes: Toward a Reflective Journalism. *Gazette: International Journal for Mass Communication Studies* 26 (2, 1980): 111–20.

——— and Robert P. Snow. 1979. *Media Logic*. Beverly Hills, Calif.: Sage.

Batscha, Robert M. 1975. *Foreign Affairs News and the Broadcast Journalist*. New York: Praeger.

Dorman, William A. and Ehsan Omeed. 1979. Reporting Iran the Shah's Way. *Columbia Journalism Review* (Jan./Feb. 1979): 27–33.

Epstein, Edward Jay. 1973. *News From Nowhere*. New York: Random House.

Heumann, Joe. 1980. U.S. Network Television: Melodrama and the Iranian Crisis. *Middle East Review* (Summer/Fall 1980): 51–55

Ismael, J.S. and T.Y. Ismael. 1980. Social Changes in Islamic Society: The Political Thought of Ayatollah Khomeini. *Social Problems* 27 (June 1980): 601–19.

Lichty, Lawrence W. and George A. Bailey. 1978. Reading the Wind: Reflections on Content Analysis of Broadcast News. In William Adams and Fay Schreibman, eds., *Television Network News: Issues in Content Research*. Washington, D.C.: School of Public and International Affairs, George Washington University.

# SUBJECT INDEX

# NAME INDEX